CONTENTMENT COMMITMENT

Live a Happier Life

A SIMPLE FRAMEWORK BY

TIM STREETER

ARBOR VINES LLC
ANN ARBOR

Copyright © 2021 Tim Streeter

All rights reserved.
Printed in the United States of America

No part of this book may be reproduced, or stored in a retrieval system, or transmitted in any form or by any means, electronic, mechanical, photocopying, recording, or otherwise, without express written permission of the publisher.

Cover photograph by Rachael Holt Photography
Author photograph by Rachael Holt Photography

Library of Congress Control Number: 1639011331

ISBN-978-1-63901-133-9 eBook
ISBN: 9798526800723 Print

Arbor Vines LLC
Ann Arbor, Michigan, United States
Contact via ContentmentCommitment.com

CONTENTS

1	*Sesame Street* | Contentment Influences	1
2	*Lost* | Contentment Commitment Origin	9
3	*The Office* | Contentment Commitment Inspiration	15
4	*Top Chef* | Contentment Commitment Ingredients	23
5	*The Big Bang Theory* | Self Dimension of Contentment	32
6	*Sex and the City* | Partner Dimension of Contentment	43
7	*This Is Us* | Dependents Dimension of Contentment	56
8	*Friends* | Friends Dimension of Contentment	71
9	*Modern Family* | Family Dimension of Contentment	83
10	*Parks and Recreation* | Community Dimension of Contentment	95
11	*Survivor* | Make The Commitment	108
12	*Glee* | Live A Happier Life	120

FOREWORD

by Ty Sassaman

Founder of The Question Project (JustOneQuestion.org)
Award-Winning Author of Just One Question: A Road Trip Memoir

What is the meaning of life?

I was asked this question by a wild-haired reveler in the very heart of craziness - a week at Burning Man festival in a stretch of desolate desert in Nevada. I was interviewing people with a single question, and "What is the meaning of life?" was this guy's response.

Upon hearing it, I instinctively responded, "Yeah, I'd love to hear the answer to that one." I wasn't intending to turn the tables, but I've heard enough hooey in my life to know what follows a question like that is either an over-eager spiritual sales pitch or the nebulous foundation to an exhausting argument. I wasn't interested in either, but this character before me - all jean jacket and John Lennon glasses - seemed sincere.

"Ok, I can tell you how I create meaning in my life," he said thoughtfully.

"Hit me," I said.

"Well, the sun comes up every day and the sun goes down every day. That's a truth that will never change. So, my challenge is living every day and making the best of it. Sleeping good at night with a clear conscience and no guilt. Watching that sun come up every day and living righteously. Doing the right thing and being with good people. That's what makes me tick."

Now, you might not have noticed - I know I didn't at the time - that the question shifted from what is the meaning of life to what *creates* meaning in life. And though it may appear subtle, the distinction is very important, and it's the reason you're holding this book at this very moment.

Tim Streeter lived the first half of his life pursuing that first question. I know that because I've known Tim most of my life. I watched him wrangle with it as he traveled through the world, searching. And, like many of us, he was unsure of what it all meant. What is the meaning of life?

But through the insecurities of youth, Tim remained steadfast in his responsibilities. He started with a paper route, attended a highly regarded college, and worked his way up the corporate ladder, eventually landing global leadership roles in Fortune 500 companies. Along the way, he got married and is now father to two awesome college-aged sons. On paper, he's lived an enviable life, one that many seek. It was not always this way.

Attempting to adapt to a convergence of major life events, fissures began to appear. Tim was disconnected from familial and friend support, and it's here that the internal shift described above happened in Tim's questioning of the world. To regain control of his own happiness, he examined his own life, assessing each dimension. And by focusing on those dimensions in which he could make positive change, he set goals and began to ask the active form of the question: What creates meaning in life?

This shift in perspective is where Tim credits the impetus of the Contentment Commitment, but in truth, it was a tool for Tim to regain the agency in his own happiness. The Contentment Commitment is no convoluted "program," nor is it dumbed-down psycho-babble intent on selling various tiers of "help." Most simply, the Contentment Commitment is a promise you make to yourself to examine your life, identify your struggles, and work to make changes. The Contentment is a result of the Commitment, just like the meaning is a result of creating it, striving for it. You get there by engaging in the process of questioning, and creating your own meaning.

I say, *Give it a shot*. And then ask, *What have you got to lose?*

INTRODUCTION

In my late 20s and early 30s, I was perceived by others to be achieving success in my professional life, but I was struggling to manage increasing demands in my personal life. I felt like I was failing as a husband, a father, and a friend, while neglecting myself as well.

In response, I leveraged existing tools designed to gain insights into happiness at work (Engagement) and evolved them to create a simple framework focused on improving happiness in life (Contentment). At first I just did it for myself, but it was such a life-changing experience that I began sharing it with select friends and colleagues struggling with similar issues. Based on their experiences and feedback, I have been sharing it ever since, and I feel a sense of pride every time I hear from someone that it has helped them to live a happier life.

Considering there is no single diet that works for everyone to manage weight (or else we would all be doing it already!), it is reasonable to expect that there is no single best approach to living a happier life that will work for everyone. There are plenty of other books out there on the topic of happiness, including some best sellers. If you are reading this one, I assume you have yet to find the approach that works best for you, and you are still searching. I hope Contentment Commitment is "the one" that helps get you where you want to go, but if not, I encourage you to keep trying new approaches until you find something that does. Or perhaps you'll take pieces of multiple ideas along with your own to create something new.

What makes the Contentment Commitment unique is how it breaks Contentment down into 6 dimensions and their sub-dimensions, asks difficult questions to help you understand what really drives your happiness in each, and then applies a proven analytical methodology to help you identify and prioritize the actions which will have the most positive effect on your life overall. It then pushes you to commit to taking those actions by formally creating accountability to yourself and others. This provides a simple and structured way to focus your efforts on achieving meaningful outcomes and takes much of the emotion out of something that is inherently deeply emotional.

The Contentment Commitment framework tends to resonate most with people who have been heavily focused on their professional lives, have new and greater responsibilities in their personal lives, and are struggling with how to make it all work. It looks well beyond the narrow lens of work-life balance and is relevant for adults of any age, regardless of what is happening in their personal and professional lives. And it works the same for any gender, ethnicity, religion, or nationality.

Of course, the framework will not instantly transport you to a constant and eternal state of perfect Contentment. If you find something that does, please let me know. What it will do is equip you with a process and tools to easily and confidently identify actions - fully in your control - that, as long as you keep your Commitment to complete them, can help you live a happier life. It isn't rocket science, so if I can share it in a compelling way, it has the potential to help anyone. If you're curious and in a place where this resonates, I invite you to jump in with both feet and see where it leads you.

Building out this framework and bringing it to life through the personal stories in the book has been a passion project years in the making. I hope it helps you and those you love live a happier life as it did for me.

CHAPTER I

Sesame Street
CONTENTMENT INFLUENCES

CONTENTMENT COMMITMENT

Big Bird, Cookie Monster, Bert and Ernie, Oscar the Grouch, and my personal favorite, the elusive Snuffleupagus (I had to look up the spelling of that one). These are only a few of the classic characters on the long-running children's television show *Sesame Street*, but each acted as a fun communication vehicle for lessons many of us were taught when we were young. The episodes tended to focus on how to help kids be smarter, stronger, and kinder, but we have all been exposed to many influences that shape our views of Contentment and how to achieve it. Hopefully, one or more of these characters sparks a memory from your childhood and will act as a portal to some deeper reflection on that time period.

Con·tent·ment: a state of happiness and satisfaction

A Look Ahead

If you're like me, it helps to have a sense of where you're going and how you're getting there. So, I'll share a sneak peek of what's coming, along with some suggestions about how to get the most out of the Contentment Commitment framework as you work your way through it.

This chapter will provide some background and context to try to get you in the right mindset. It will push you to think about how your experiences growing up have influenced your thoughts on Contentment. There will be a lot of questions, a lot of reflection, and possibly a point where you will wonder, where is this going? So, let me preempt that question.

Chapters 2 and 3 reveal more detail around the convergence of life events which led to the need for me to make changes, and the inspiration for the creation of the framework itself. The good news is you'll get a break from all of the questions here, but the bad news is that it may feel a bit one-sided as I share how I was feeling and why I responded the way I did.

Then in Chapter 4, I'll share a high-level overview of the ingredients of the Contentment Commitment framework you'll use to identify, prioritize, and commit to the changes which will have the most positive effect on helping you live a happier life. Here, we will introduce the 6 dimensions of Contentment as well as the tools and process which will help stimulate and organize your thoughts around them. And then we go deep. Real deep.

Chapters 5 through 10 explore each of the 6 dimensions and the sub-dimensions within them. When you get to this part, I recommend no more than one chapter per day. Why? Because there are a lot of questions. Like, *a lot* of questions. And some of them are hard questions. This technique is not meant to make your brain hurt, but to expose you to all the different variables that influence your happiness and help you figure out which ones matter the most to you. Focusing on one dimension of Contentment per day will give you time to *really* think about it, and it will keep you from getting confused about which sub-dimensions were included and what exactly they meant, etc.

I also *highly* recommend using the worksheets referenced while you are focused on an individual dimension. Each chapter will explain the sub-dimensions and provide examples to bring them to life. When these are fresh in your mind, along with the ideas you generate as you answer the tough questions, it is the best time to capture your ratings, rankings, and actions which could improve your satisfaction. You can always revisit them and update later, but the idea is to document your thoughts while you are deeply engaged with them.

Throughout these chapters, I will be sharing personal stories to try to encourage you to reflect openly and deeply. I do this not because I think you need or want to know all of the details of my life, but because if I am going to encourage you to go all in, I figure I should be doing the same with you. If the examples become too much for you, then just jump ahead to the next section. No hard feelings - I won't even know unless you tell me.

You will also likely notice some overlap on some of the sub-dimensions. In real life, our experiences don't all map perfectly to just one category, so don't worry if an action you've identified is in the "right" dimension. Remember, the point is to reflect on different aspects of each of the 6 dimensions of Contentment, and to consider what brings you happiness, what you'd like to do more, and what you'd like to do less. It's not important that we categorize them in a perfectly consistent way.

Once you have completed your journey through the 6 dimensions of Contentment, focusing on no more than one per day, you'll then take a step back and hopefully pat yourself on the back. You'll have a view of which subdimensions are most important for you to improve right now, your satisfaction in each, and a list of actions you have identified which would improve your ratings. With all of that as input, you'll then rate your satisfaction in each of the dimensions overall and rank what is most important to improve overall. This will inform your priorities and help you narrow the list down to the three to five actions that will help you the most. You will then formally commit to them with a contract with someone you trust as a witness.

And then, assuming you complete the actions to which you have committed, you will be on the path to living a happier life. You may run through the cycle once or you may run through it multiple times depending on your timelines, how well it is working for you, and the amount of change you are seeking.

A final note: you will notice that each chapter is anchored to a TV show. I did this not to date myself with my selections, but rather to connect the framework to something practical and relatable since self-help concepts can often come across as overly academic or technical. It's not necessary to know the shows or the characters referenced to work through the process, and I'll provide a brief explanation of each one in case it is new to you. There is a surprising amount of wisdom in these sources of entertainment when you look beyond the surface.

A Look Back

Some of the most common origins of our definitions of Contentment include where we grew up, how we were raised, our experience at school, and our friends, relatives, and communities. Before we can discuss how to live a happier life, it is important to reflect on some of the things that influence our definitions and question them. Warning: it's about to start raining questions, but remember … the best way to get answers is to ask questions!

Let's start with where you grew up. Did you grow up in an urban, suburban, or rural area? What was the weather like? Could you see water, mountains, or fields? Were you taught that success was getting out of the place where you were born or staying there to help the people who raised you? Were you mainly in one or two places, or were you frequently moving to new places? What did the previous generations of your family do? Did they seem happy with their choices? How has this affected your views of the ideal place to live?

Who raised you? Did you have two parents, one parent, no parents? Were you raised by extended family or step-parents? Did those who raised you seem to enjoy parenting or view it as a burden? Did they support you financially and emotionally? Did they emphasize the importance of school? Did they encourage you to try new things and attend activities and events? How has this shaped your views of what it means to be a good parent?

What was your schooling like? Did you attend public or private school? What was the ethnic diversity of the student population? How many years did you attend? What level of education were you expected to achieve? What did you actually achieve? Did you have teachers who encouraged you to push yourself? Did you have coaches who made you better? How has this helped define your views of the kind of experience you would want for your kids (whether you have or intend to have kids or not)?

What types of friends did you have? Did you prioritize quantity over quality or the opposite? Were you drawn to people more similar to you or more different from you? What did you do to support them? What did they do to support you? How long were they your friends? Which friends have you kept the longest and why? How have these experiences influenced your definition of what it means to be a good friend?

What was your relationship with your grandparents? Do you have any siblings? How often did you see your aunts, uncles, cousins, and other extended family? Did you see some more than others? Did they live close or far away? What role did they play in raising you? How did your parents (or others who raised you) view them? Which relatives did you most enjoy spending time with? Why? Which relatives did you least enjoy spending time with? Why? How does this affect your views on the importance of relatives and your definition of what it means to be a good family member?

What was the sense of community where you were raised? What images come to mind when you think of the word community? Were people more proud of their city/town or their neighborhoods within it? How integrated or divided was the community by economic or social characteristics? Did people tend to band together or fight with each other? Did people seem to care more about themselves or helping others? Did people seem to care about those outside of their community or more focused on protecting their own? Were their sports teams or tourist attractions that were a sense of pride for everyone? How does this make you feel about the type of community you would want to live in?

Ok, that's probably enough questions for now. The purpose is to stimulate your thinking and help you better understand what makes you feel happy and why. To illustrate the value of reflecting on these questions, I will share my own answers and how they have influenced the definitions of Contentment I had while I was growing up. After all, if I'm going to ask you to do some deep reflection to answer some hard questions, I probably should lead by example.

Allow myself to introduce ... myself

Sorry, that's one of my favorite quotes from the original Austin Powers movie, and I couldn't resist using it.

Hi, my name is Tim. I was born and raised in Kalamazoo, Michigan - a mid-size city halfway between Detroit and Chicago. We lived in a middle class, mostly white neighborhood full of families. I lived in the same house until I left for college. I was thankful to have stability, safety, and lots of kids to play with. But I also wished that the neighborhood was more diverse like the schools I attended; I only got to see some of my friends from school in my neighborhood. I told myself that if I ever had kids, I would want them to grow up in one place without having to deal with a new house, new school, and new friends. I would want them to be able to go outside and play with whoever else happened to be out and feel safe. I would want them to see all different kinds of people in the neighborhood, learn from them, and appreciate the differences.

I was raised by two parents who were married in their early 20s and never experienced divorce or separation. They have now been married for over 50 years! They supported me financially, expected I would go to college, and expected they would pay for it. They supported all of my activities and came to nearly every soccer game I ever had while I was growing up (and many I had as an adult). When I was young, I heard them argue enough to know that it wasn't all rainbows and butterflies, but I believe their love has grown over time. I thought if I was ever married, I would want to smile and laugh more often and argue as little as possible.

I attended public schools in Kalamazoo and loved it. All the way through, the student population was representative of the ethnic mix of the city, and I met a lot of people I would never have been able to meet if I had attended private school. I am certain this is where I learned to love R&B music and get comfortable dancing like nobody's watching. I was fortunate to be part of the charter class of the Kalamazoo Area Math & Science Center, which brought together the district's best teachers and students, and allowed me to experience a more college-like learning environment for half of the day without giving up what I valued about my experiences the other half. I always had good grades and was told I was smart, but that experience helped me realize there are a lot of people waaaaay smarter than me and super interesting in different ways. I had some great coaches and some terrible coaches, and I remember how each made the experience more or less fun. I knew that if I ever had kids, I would want them to go to a large public school to have some of these same experiences and befriend all different kinds of people.

On the topic of friends, I seemed to have different groups of people for different activities. I was drawn to people with similar interests in some cases, but I was also fascinated by those that were completely different. I enjoyed being able to go to parties and always find a person or small group that I knew well enough to hang out with. At the same time, I am only in contact with a couple of people I called friends in high school, so I look more to my college experience to shape my view of what it means to be a good friend. In high school, it seemed like we were all trying to be cool and fit in without really knowing much about ourselves or each other, whereas in college, I was more confident about the kind of person I wanted to be and the kinds of friendships I valued. What being a good friend meant to me continued to evolve as I had new life experiences like working, moving, getting married, and having kids.

I feel lucky to have had one set of parents, two sets of grandparents, one older brother, two sets of aunts and uncles, and five cousins. And I got to see them all. Some more than others for various reasons, but I was able to spend time with all of them because my parents prioritized it. I also gained new sets of all of those when my wife and I were married, and I feel thankful for them as well. They are a much larger family, so we do not get to see all of them, but they definitely make life more interesting. I feel most grateful for the relatives I have known, both as a child and my adult life, as we know things about each other most people don't. I am certain these experiences have influenced how I value family now, and shape the kinds of experiences we try to provide for our kids.

My hometown had two public high schools, a community college, a college, and a university. This provided many opportunities to attend sporting and cultural events. I felt proud about Kalamazoo then and I think the city has only gotten better since. The schools and businesses provided a representative mix of the population, but the neighborhoods were more segregated. We had semi-pro sports teams but none that I would say united the whole community. Nowadays, there is pride in the Kalamazoo Promise, which was the first time a community committed to pay for college for all graduating high school students. And being the hometown of New York Yankees baseball star Derek Jeter, many take pride in that as well.

CONTENTMENT COMMITMENT

Your Contentment

All of this detail is not meant to bore you like a person talking too much about themselves on a first date. Rather, it is meant to highlight how the experiences we have had growing up, and the beliefs of the people with whom we spent the most time, have influenced our definitions of Contentment. This does not make them correct or incorrect, so it is important that you reflect on them, question them, and, if necessary, update them to reflect your full life experience to date.

"Yeah, well, I've got a dream too, but it's about singing and dancing and making people happy. That's the kind of dream that gets better the more people you share it with."
-- Kermit the Frog from *Sesame Street*

Your Commitment

1. Reflect on the experiences you've had that have contributed to your definition of Contentment.
2. Are they yours or someone else's? Have they changed over time or remained the same?
3. No need to document your responses, but make sure you've spent some time thinking about them and have some clarity around it before moving on.

CHAPTER 2

Lost
CONTENTMENT COMMITMENT ORIGIN

CONTENTMENT COMMITMENT

If you're unfamiliar with the TV series *Lost*, it follows the lives of a group of plane crash survivors on a mysterious tropical island, but metaphorically, it is about people who are lost and searching for meaning and purpose in their lives … at least, I *think* it was, as it was a pretty confusing show at times. In that spirit, it seems like a good analogy to explain how I was feeling when the idea of Contentment Commitment was first conceived.

Just entering my 30s, I had been working at Accenture for 10 years and had been continuously taking on larger roles. If you've never heard of Accenture, it is a global company which advises other companies of all sizes on how to improve their strategies, processes, and technologies to drive better business results, and then helps them do it. I felt proud that during that time, I had been promoted from Analyst to Consultant to Manager to Senior Manager, and I expanded my scope from local to regional to global roles. My aspiration then was to be promoted to the next and highest level: Managing Director.

When I reflect on that time period, it is clear that my ambition was based more on what I had learned growing up and others' definition of success. In high school, the focus was on getting the best grades and excelling in as many extracurriculars as possible so that I could get into the best university. Once in college, the focus was again on getting the best grades and having as many relevant internship experiences as possible so I could get a job at a top employer. And once I began working, the goal was to progress as far as possible as quickly as possible. I understood that to be the definition of success in professional life, and presumed that with success would come happiness.

At the same time, I was also taking on more in my personal life. I was married at 24, we had our first child at 28, and had our second child when I was 31. In addition, as people who grew up in Michigan but despised winter, my wife and I had just moved to Tampa, Florida, and believed that was the place we would raise our children and spend the rest of our lives. I was doing everything I thought was expected of me. I graduated from a great college, I secured a good job, I got married, and I had kids.

So, why didn't I *feel* happy? It turns out there were many reasons.

I felt like I was failing as a husband

Before we were parents, it was just the two of us. We would have elaborate date nights, sleep in the next day, and I would cook breakfast for us as we lazily eased into the morning. We would go on walks and watch TV shows, and take vacations to relax and explore together. And we rarely ever argued about anything.

Then, after we had kids, it seemed it was nearly entirely the opposite. We were arguing frequently, and over things that in and of themselves were unimportant. We were constantly tired and each of us suspected that the other had a much better/easier parenting role than the other. I couldn't remember the last time we had tried to do something fun for just the two of us. But our parents were far away, we were in a new city, and we didn't yet have a babysitter we felt we could trust with such small children. In our desire to try to be the best parents ever, we seemed to have forgotten about each other. And with frequent travel and long hours at work, it was hard to see how things were going to change anytime in the foreseeable future.

I felt like I was failing as a parent

Since before I had kids, I aspired to be a parent that was an equal partner. I wanted to carry my weight when the kids woke up in the middle of the night. I wanted to change the diapers and feed them as much as my wife did. I wanted to play with them whenever they asked me to. I wanted to take them on walks and watch them marvel at all the things I had stopped noticing. I had prioritized working from home since before they were born so all of this would be possible.

Instead, I was missing it. The first 9 weeks of my younger son's life, I flew from Tampa to Los Angeles on Monday and back on Friday. The. First. 9. Weeks. I knew from my experience with our older son how much kids change in the first weeks and months, and yet, somehow, I was missing it. Not only that, my wife was left to handle all of the feeding, diapers, naps, baths, and waking in the night without me. I was feeling increased pressure to perform at work and she must have felt like I was having an easy vacation from life at home. Not to mention I was missing time with my older son, too, who was 3 at the time.

I felt like I was failing as a friend

I was used to having many friends in high school and college. I had observed the natural filtering that happens when you are the first one in your group to get married. It becomes easier and more logical to hang out with your spouse and other couples than go out with single friends who are looking to "hook up" at the bars. There is an even bigger filtering out when you are the first to have kids.

I realized that I can be absolutely entranced watching every movement and facial expression of my kids, while others can only fake interest for a short time. This tends to filter out not only the single friends, but also the fun married couples without kids.

Next thing I know, we are only hanging out with other couples with young kids. While I do think this is a natural transition, I also had long-time friends who I wanted to continue being friends with. I learned during this time to prioritize friends who actually took time to meet our kids and play with them a bit rather than trying to pretend we were back in school with no real responsibilities. I knew it wasn't fair to only see them when they came to visit us, but when and where else would I have time to see them?

I felt like I was failing to stay connected to family

We moved to Florida to escape winter forever. But my parents, my in-laws, and our only siblings were all living in Michigan, and we had the only grandchildren on either side of the family. As a result, we felt we had to spend every vacation going back to Michigan so they could have time with our kids and we could have time with them. But I also had cousins and aunts and uncles in New York and Oregon. We used to see them every one or two years, but now the gaps were being stretched. Even though it felt like we were giving all of our vacation time to this group, we were somehow having less time with them than before. I felt guilty if we didn't go back to visit, but I also longed to travel for pleasure to places other than Michigan.

I felt like I was failing to contribute meaningfully to my community

Both of my parents and my only sibling were all public school teachers and have positively influenced the lives of hundreds of kids. My wife has a Masters of Social Work and had roles as a child therapist and advocating for the elderly, so I saw her also helping hundreds of people. I had always felt that it was enough to make money to support our family, and I justified this as enabling her to focus on more meaningful pursuits that are rewarded less financially. I found myself questioning the societal value of helping a large company that already makes billions of dollars increase revenue and profitability.

All of this had a negative effect on my productivity and engagement at work, which had been the one part of my life where I still felt I was achieving some success.

That's when it hit me. I realized that if I was achieving success by others'

LOST

definitions but feeling unhappy, it was time for me to create my own definitions and make some changes. After all, no one knows what makes you happy more than you.

CONTENTMENT COMMITMENT

Your Contentment

What's your story? What experience have you had that made you question how you are using your time personally or professionally? Where are you trying to go? How will you get there? What made you start reading this book?

"A leader can't lead 'til he knows where he's going."
-- John Locke from *Lost*

Your Commitment

1. Reflect on the experiences you've had that contributed to your definition of Success.
2. How would you describe the relationship between Success and Contentment? Have there been any events in your life that caused you to question it?
3. Again, no need to document your responses, but make sure you've spent some time thinking about them and have some clarity around it before moving on.

CHAPTER 3

The Office
CONTENTMENT COMMITMENT INSPIRATION

CONTENTMENT COMMITMENT

I'm thankful that my work experiences at Accenture and Whirlpool had very little in common with the Dunder-Mifflin Paper Company from the television show *The Office*, and I realize that professional life may seem like a strange place for inspiration for improving our personal lives. At the same time, employers invest millions of dollars every year for the purpose of improving happiness at work (more formally referred to as Employee Engagement) and understanding the link to human performance and productivity. So it stands to reason that there must be some useful tools to leverage somewhere in our professional lives.

I was first introduced to the concept of Personal Engagement in the early 2000s by a colleague who was piloting something he had created with his team. I assumed it was a third party tool, but later learned it is more of an idea for people to interpret than one specific tool for all to follow. This is validated by a simple Google search of "Personal Engagement," which returns dozens of variations on the theme without a single common source of origin. Maybe it's best that way - it fits nicely with my philosophy that there are always multiple ways to achieve an objective. I modified and evolved the concept to fit my needs, and am sharing some detail about my version of it here to highlight the elements that were most influential in the design of the Contentment Commitment framework.

What struck me about the concept originally was how such a simplistic approach could yield such powerful insights. If you've ever supervised others and conducted a performance review, you likely have been exposed to different types of employees. On one extreme is the person who is unhappy with everything all the time and you risk spending a disproportionate amount of your time with them vs. other team members. At the other extreme is the employee who is happy with everything and doesn't seem to need or want any support. If they really are that happy, I want to know why, so I can replicate the approach with others. Of course, most employees are between these two extremes.

Insights into Happiness at Work

So, what is Personal Engagement and how does it work? I thought you might ask that. It is a framework which includes 6 dimensions of professional life and guides the individual to rank the importance and their satisfaction with each. Essentially, it is asking about happiness at work, which is more formally referred

THE OFFICE

to as Employee Engagement. The dimensions are Work, People, Opportunities, Rewards, Balance, and Values. We'll explore each of the dimensions to help you better understand the process and insights.

But first, an easy way to think about it is this: we all want to have only the most interesting work AND only work with competent people we respect AND get that promotion we deserve AND make more money AND work less hours AND do it all at a place we are proud to be a part of. However, it is extremely unlikely that all of these things will happen at the same time, so we need to think about which are most important to focus on at a moment in time. We must also realize that while the relative priorities do not change daily, they definitely change over time, especially as we experience major events in our personal and professional lives.

Let's think about the Work dimension first. This refers to the actual work you do. For example, when someone hired to be a programmer is treated more like a personal assistant, it might result in high dissatisfaction in this dimension. Someone in a very niche role doing what they were hired to do but longing to learn new or different skills may have some dissatisfaction. And someone who feels that their role has little or no impact on the organization's results might long for work they view as being more valued.

In the People dimension, employees are asked to think about others with whom they work most closely. The oft-used phrase "people leave bosses not employers" speaks to the supervisor aspect that most think of first. However, it is also very important to feel a sense of belonging to a team or group that is trying to achieve a common goal. And for those with direct reports, it is important to feel confident in their abilities and trust them to execute on your behalf. Positive people can make the most mundane tasks fun, and negative people can make the most interesting work miserable.

Opportunities are most commonly associated with career progression or having a chance to earn promotion to a higher level, achieve tenure, or expand responsibility in some way. How likely it is and how quickly it is expected to happen can impact satisfaction in this dimension. Opportunities also refer to having the chance to move into other parts of the organization. Someone who got a "foot in the door" in one part of the organization may aspire to move to a different part they really wanted to join in the first place. Sometimes this can refer to having the opportunity to be exposed to different leaders who are the "decision makers" as well.

The first thought in the Rewards dimension is typically compensation or how much money someone is paid to do the job. At some point, nearly everyone feels they should be paid more or were disappointed they got little or no raise. Perhaps you are happy with your compensation, but feel you get little or no recognition from your supervisors, which leaves you feeling under-appreciated. Benefits are another aspect of Rewards. Someone who feels that they do not have enough time away or are having higher than expected deductions from their paycheck might also have low satisfaction scores.

Balance is most commonly associated with Work/Life balance and can be very subjective. I have seen people working a high number of hours who rate their satisfaction very high and people working part-time who rate their satisfaction very low. It is much more related to what other demands you may have on your time than the number of hours in your work week. The most dissatisfaction in this dimension typically comes from people who feel that work is inhibiting their ability to spend time focused on their family, friends, or themselves.

Values is a broad category, but a simple way to think of it is to ask yourself "Am I proud to work for this organization?" If you're at a party and somebody asks you where you work, are you eager to share, or are you trying to change the subject as quickly as possible? For some, this is more associated with what the products or services the employer provides - for example, making medicine or making cigarettes. For others, it is more about the ethics or social agenda of the organization - for example, do you trust the leaders to practice what they preach in relation to gender equality, racial equality, and sustainability? And for others, it is more about how much an organization gives back to the communities in which its people work and live. Dissatisfaction is most common when there is a difference between your values and your organization's values.

Ranking these dimensions from 1 to 6 is much more difficult than you might imagine. Aren't they all important? Of course, but if you could only get one of them right in your first or next job, which is most important to you right now? I have literally seen every dimension listed as #1 and every dimension listed as #6 on people's rankings. And by the way, there are no ties. You cannot have a 3-way tie for top priority. This is the part that forces people to think beyond "I want all of them to be 10 on a 10-point scale all of the time." While that is aspirational, it is unrealistic and sets up both the supervisor and employee to fail.

For early career professionals, Opportunities and Rewards tend to be the focus. For those who choose to get married and/or have children, or those caring for aging parents or relatives, Balance starts to become more important. For those in the latter part of their careers, Work and People tend to move to the forefront. For some, Values is consistently top or consistently bottom of their lists, regardless of what's happening in their personal or professional lives. And these are broad generalizations with many individuals breaking the trends. There is no right or wrong - only improved clarity about what needs attention.

As I customized the tool and started using it with my direct reports, I was amazed to learn that even though I was speaking with them daily and thought I was in tune with how they were feeling, frequently someone was much more happy or unhappy than I thought in a particular dimension. Often there was something happening outside of work that was impacting their happiness at work. While Engagement is the preferred word to allude to happiness at work, the manifestation of this in business outcome is performance and productivity.

As you can imagine, this sparked many useful discussions. It was very clear that happiness outside of work had the potential to influence happiness at work and vice versa. And it was very clear that the happier someone was in both their professional and personal life, the better they performed at work. I found that I thoroughly enjoyed having conversations that started with a focus of improving performance at work but ended up having a broader positive effect on someone's life outside of work.

Even with all of these great discussions, I still felt that something was missing from the process. It was as if we had discovered together what was causing dissatisfaction and agreed it required attention, but we had no action plan to address it. So, I added a new component to the tool. For the top one or two dimensions requiring attention, I asked the individual to come up with two or three actions they could take that would improve their satisfaction that were completely under their control. Then, I added two or three actions I could take as their supervisor that would improve their satisfaction in each dimension. And we committed to each other to take these actions in advance of our next review.

Not surprisingly, this approach led to improvement in their satisfaction of those dimensions nearly every single time. The only outliers were when someone failed to keep their commitment to take the actions under their control, or if they had a major event in their personal or professional lives which shifted their priorities. While it was disappointing to see when it happened, it also changed the dynamic from them feeling unsupported to feeling like it was ultimately up to them to prioritize the actions required to improve their satisfaction. I continued to evolve the methodology by weighting the dimensions to produce an overall score, and I set objectives for myself as a supervisor to help each of my direct reports gain this self-awareness and improve their overall satisfaction across all the dimensions.

This was so powerful for me that I continued to use the approach with every direct report I had for the remainder of my career, in addition to the company's official performance management process. I consistently had team members tell me that they had never looked at their happiness at work in this way, and that they felt more knowledgeable and empowered to take control of it than they ever had before. Beyond helping them improve their performance at work, I felt like I was helping them improve their happiness in their professional lives, and it felt great.

Executive Coaching ... or was that therapy?

Around the same time, there was another experience from the office that served as a major inspiration. In my drive to be promoted to the highest level at Accenture as quickly as possible, I had a setback. The first year I was eligible for promotion, I did not achieve it. I was very angry and felt my contributions were not being valued as much as they should be. My response was to seek out the most senior person I knew in the organization - Raul Alvarado, head of the Operations Council, who oversaw the COOs of all the different parts of the company. I asked him to be my sponsor and champion my promotion in the next cycle.

I'll never forget his answer. He said, "No, I'm not going to do that ... but I *will* help you." He had someone on retainer that he used for Executive Coaching for two or three people each year and agreed to sponsor weekly sessions for me for a full year. I did not ask for Executive Coaching, and frankly, I did not think I needed any, but I also respected his leadership style and he said he had

THE OFFICE

benefited from the same, so I agreed to give it a try. My wife, the social worker, would quickly recognize this coaching as therapy at work.

The sessions started with some practical skills, such as how to influence others and negotiate more effectively. Then, they seemed to move in a different direction when the topic of concise communications morphed into a Language of Inclusion and my coach began to make connections about how what we *say* affects how we *think* and *feel*. Specifically, choosing words that describe what something is (rather than what it is not) is not only more concise and direct, but it also requires you to assess situations for what they are rather than what they are not, which has the effect of making you feel that you are noticing more positive things and fewer negative things. Whaaaat?

As our conversations started to focus on desired outcomes of the experience, I initially continued to focus on how to leverage these new skills to impress the right people to get noticed and get promoted. But then my Executive Coach asked me, "*Why* do you want to get promoted? What will change in your life once this is achieved? And how will it help address the things that make you feel like you are failing outside of work?" Essentially, he was asking if I knew what actually made me happy. Dammit, this *was* therapy at work. And I didn't have great answers to those questions, which I suppose was the point. Thank you, Dr. JM Perry, for this enlightening experience.

While there were many positive outcomes from these sessions, including a transformation in the way I thought, spoke, and wrote, there was one lesson learned that was more fundamental and more important than all of the rest. Maybe, *just maybe*, being promoted as far as possible as quickly as possible isn't what will make me happy in my professional and personal life.

Equipped with this new self-awareness and a framework for how to better understand and improve happiness at work, I started to wonder if a similar approach could help me better understand and improve happiness in my personal life. And so began the idea of the Contentment Commitment.

CONTENTMENT COMMITMENT

Your Contentment

Whether you have been exposed to any tools that were meant to help with your happiness at work (Engagement) or not, I encourage you to spend a few minutes on the exercise below. At a minimum, it will give you some practice rating and ranking various dimensions - which is harder than you might think. At best, it will provide you with new insights to share with your supervisor about which dimensions are most influential on your happiness at work, and what specific actions could help improve it.

"I talk a lot, so I've learned to tune myself out."
-- Kelly Kapoor from *The Office*

Your Commitment

1. Download the R3 Worksheets at **ContentmentCommitment.com/Tools** and pull out the one focused on *Personal Engagement - Happiness at Work*.
2. For your current or most recent job, rate each of the 6 dimensions (Work, People, Opportunities, Rewards, Balance, and Values) on a scale of 1 (least satisfied) to 10 (most satisfied), then rank them based on what is most important to improve right now.
3. For the dimensions you rated most important to improve, list one or two actions entirely in your control which could help improve your satisfaction.
4. If you're feeling adventurous, share it with your supervisor.

CHAPTER 4

Top Chef
CONTENTMENT COMMITMENT INGREDIENTS

CONTENTMENT COMMITMENT

In my professional life, I often used the analogy of a chef to explain my role in Talent Acquisition (aka Recruiting) to others. To oversimplify, top chefs gather ingredients that are available to everyone and combine them in a unique way to create something which diners have never experienced before. They pay great attention to which ingredients they choose, how menu items are prepared and presented, and to the needs and preferences of the people they are serving.

In the world of Talent Acquisition, there were many potential "ingredients" available to everyone, such as Applicant Tracking Systems, Candidate Relationship Management tools, Employee Referral tools, Technical and Behavioral Assessment tools, Skills Matching AI tools, Natural Language Processing tools to support candidate outreach, and many more. Not every company needs every tool, and some tools are a better fit to an organization's technical architecture or culture. The value of someone in my role was to understand what was needed for a company in that moment of its business lifecycle, then gather the best ingredients available and combine them in a unique way to create a custom "dish" for the purpose of driving targeted outcomes.

In my personal life, the same analogy works in relation to how my brother and I create music. There are many potential ingredients available to everyone, such as music editing software, instruments, loops, lyrics, vocals, etc. What makes a song unique is how the producers, writers, and musicians work together to combine these things in a way that no one has ever done before. Just like with a chef, not every patron will enjoy every dish, but this is not the objective. The purpose of creating a song is to express a personal feeling or message.

The Contentment Commitment is also a gathering of ingredients that are available to everyone but combined in a unique way to create a custom tool for the purpose of driving a specific outcome: to help people better understand what makes them happy, identify specific actions they can take to improve their happiness, and commit to doing it. Or, more directly, to help you live a happier life. I felt that if I combined the principles and values from my Executive Coaching experience with the framework and insights from the Personal Engagement tool - and evolved it a bit - there might be something very powerful.

If Engagement measures happiness in your professional life, then let's think of Contentment as a way to measure happiness in your life overall. Similar to the

6 dimensions of professional life represented in Personal Engagement, we'll focus on 6 dimensions of Contentment: Self, Partner, Dependents, Friends, Family, Community. There is nothing scientifically relevant or magical about having 6 dimensions as far as I am aware. If you felt it was important to include additional dimensions, you could easily adjust the approach to include more. If not all of the dimensions are relevant in your life currently, you can of course skip one or more of them. I kept it at 6 because I felt that number worked well with Personal Engagement, and I was able to come up with a list of 6 personal dimensions which I felt covered the vast majority of factors that drive happiness in our personal lives.

Despite having been out of consulting for several years, my brain continues to function with a consulting mindset. This means I'll equip you with some user-friendly tools and templates to help guide you through the process. By the time you're done reading, you will know how to use R3 Worksheets, the Priority Matrix, and C3 Forms to organize and document your thoughts. And you will be amazed at how they help make something so complex seem so simple.

Reflect on 6 dimensions of Contentment

The first step in the Contentment Commitment is to reflect on each dimension of Contentment. The next several chapters will help you do this in a meaningful and holistic way. We'll share examples, situations, and we'll get into sub-dimensions and maybe even sub-sub-dimensions. If that sounds scary, don't worry - we'll avoid the temptation to over-engineer the tool and focus on this process as a source of thought and inspiration rather than a strict script to follow. There are quotes attributed to Albert Einstein and Steve Jobs with a

CONTENTMENT COMMITMENT

similar philosophy, but I prefer the phrasing in this anonymous quote: "it is simple to create something complex and complex to create something simple." While there are some complexities behind the scenes, the Contentment Commitment should feel very simple to the people using it.

As you start to reflect on each dimension, you will think about which aspects of each are going well and make you feel happy. It's important to recognize these and continue them. In addition, you will think about which aspects are going poorly and make you feel guilty or as though you are failing in some aspect of your life. It's not just about fixing things that are broken, but also about recognizing and prioritizing things that are working. In the corporate world, this is akin to the performance management concept that your productivity and engagement will improve more by capitalizing on your strengths than by focusing only on your "opportunities for improvement" (remember, you can't say "weaknesses" at work).

To help you with this part, you can leverage the R3 Worksheets, which provide a simple way to Reflect, Rate & Rank each of the 6 dimensions of Contentment. You will also be able to capture your ideas for actions that could improve your satisfaction in the same place.

Rate Satisfaction

After thinking through all the different aspects of a dimension, you will rate each one on a scale of 1 to 10. A score of 1 means you are unable to think of any hypothetical situation that could make it worse than it already is. A score of 10 means it is so perfect right now there is nothing that could make it any better. It is quite unusual to be at either extreme, and in between, there is a lot of space for you to consider how you're feeling right now.

Keep in mind, there are a couple of objectives in assigning these satisfaction ratings. The first is to help you understand which dimensions may be in better or worse shape relative to each other. For example, if you rate Family a 7 and Self a 3, and identify actions you can take to improve in each, you might prioritize committing to those that improve your Satisfaction in the Self dimension, since your satisfaction with Family is already in a decent place. The second objective is to establish a baseline, so that after you commit to taking actions to improve, and then rate your satisfaction again in the future, you can see if it has the desired result.

I have not developed a scale to prescribe exactly what each number means, as people tend to create their own definitions between the extremes and that's ok.

We are not trying to achieve a "perfect score" and declare victory. Rather, we are trying to maintain a pulse of how we are feeling in each dimension as we keep trying new things to live a happier life and make adjustments as we experience changes over time. An easy way to illustrate this is to think about how satisfaction ratings may change for someone who is in their first year as a new parent vs. their ratings in the previous year. It is quite common in this situation for people to focus 100% of their energy on trying to be great parents while unintentionally sacrificing everything else.

Rank the Importance to Improve Right Now

Once you have rated your satisfaction in each dimension, you will rank them. This is where people can sometimes get stuck thinking "I have to put Family first and Self last or else it means I am selfish or don't love my family." This is not the purpose. Similarly, I have had individuals ask me, "How can I say that my spouse is more important than my kids, or my kids are more important than my spouse?" This is also not the purpose of this exercise, and it's a common reason people try to list 2-3 dimensions as all being #1.

Instead, think of these rankings as evaluating which areas have the potential to make you most happy. In other words, if you could only get one of them to be a 10, which one would you choose? Then, among the remaining five dimensions, which would you choose, and so on. In this way, you are not saying one is more important than another, rather you are simply saying that one is more important to focus on *right now* to improve your happiness overall.

For example, I may have rated Partner a 3 if I feel like I am not being as good a husband as I want to be and Community a 3 if I feel like I am not doing enough to connect with the community in which I live. I care about both, but if I can only make an improvement in one of them, which one is more important to me *right now*? Keep in mind, these can change over time. In this case, I might conclude that my marriage is the more urgent priority, and the opportunity to get more involved in my community will still be there once I am happy I am making improvements in the Partner dimension. The opposite approach puts my marriage at risk, and it may no longer be there to improve.

Another common example I see are couples who have kids under the age of 3. There is often a catalyst during this period when one or both parents feel like they never do anything for each other or for themselves anymore, and they start to wonder how they can be great parents *and* still do some of the things they used to enjoy. If I have limited free time, should I focus it on trying to be a better husband or improving on my own physical health? Which is more important to me *right now*? I highly recommend openly discussing these questions with others that are impacted by your decisions to make sure you're in sync. In this example, you may discover that your partner also wants to prioritize their physical health, and something as simple as taking daily walks together might improve both dimensions.

A third example is someone who has moved away from their hometown and started a new job. They may naturally be very focused on getting settled at work, making friends, and getting connected to their new community. During this time, they may deprioritize going back to their hometown to visit family. It does not mean they do not love their family anymore, it just means there is already a high satisfaction with that dimension, and it is more important *right now* to focus on actions that can improve Contentment in other dimensions.

We'll come back to this later, but hopefully this helps clarify the purpose of ranking the relative importance at a moment in time based on current levels of satisfaction and life circumstances vs. an absolute ranking that stays constant over time.

Identify & Prioritize Actions

Once you have rated each dimension from 1 (most important to improve) to 6 (least important to improve), you will then think about actions you can take that would improve your satisfaction in each dimension. You will focus on actions that are completely under your control so that sole accountability for completing them sits with you.

This is the fun part where you get to think about all of the things you wish you had time to do but haven't been able to prioritize. Many times, there is one headline action, but I encourage you to take the time to think through many possibilities, as there are always multiple actions you can take that will improve your happiness. For this part, you'll let the ideas flow and write down whatever comes to mind, however big or small it may be. You should have at least 3 actions for each dimension, so if your list is shorter, it means you should spend more time thinking about it or perhaps solicit input from someone close to you for additional idea generation.

It is important to break down general actions into measurable ones. For example, "get fit" or "improve health" is not particularly measurable. However, "exercise 30 minutes per day for 3 days per week" is. An action to "visit family more" creates the possibility that you will complete the action but still feel guilty you are not visiting enough, therefore failing to improve your satisfaction in that dimension. An action to "visit my parents at their house once every 3 months" is defining up front what level is required to improve your satisfaction and ensures that if you achieve it, you will have a higher rating.

Once you have a good list of actions you could take that would improve your satisfaction in each dimension, we will narrow it down to the top 3 for each. This is where the Priority Matrix will help you decide which ones to choose based on impact and ability to achieve. For example, if two actions would have a similar positive effect but one of them will take half of the time or effort, I recommend prioritizing the one that takes half the time. Or one action may have a more significant effect on your overall satisfaction, but you are not confident about your ability to complete it. A good guide in this case is to focus on actions that are "aggressive but achievable."

After you have narrowed the list down to the top 3 in each dimension, you can sit back and marvel at what you have accomplished. You will have a list of almost 20 actions you can take - entirely in your control - that will make you happier if you actually do them! Many people never take the time to reflect on what makes them happy and therefore don't even know what they could do to improve the situation. They are often working hard to try to improve, but not in a smart way. This leads to failure to complete the goals at all or still feeling unhappy after completing them, because the prioritized actions were not the ones which will improve overall satisfaction most significantly.

At this stage, we'll look across all of the actions you have listed and overlay your ratings of which dimensions are most important to improve right now. The goal is to pick at least three actions but not more than five that will have the biggest impact on improving your Contentment. I recommend this range because taking fewer than three actions may not provide a noticeable improvement in your overall happiness, and trying to do more than five at once increases the risk that you will be unable to complete them and be left feeling unsatisfied.

The same Priority Matrix that helps guide you to your top few possible actions in each dimension will also help guide your selection of the top three to five overall across all of the dimensions. It's good like that.

Commit to Change

Everything up to this point has been about helping you *understand* and *prioritize* what drives your Contentment. The final step of the Contentment Commitment process will be to formally *commit* to taking the actions you identified that will have the biggest impact. To increase the probability that you

CONTENTMENT COMMITMENT

will complete the actions you have identified and reap the benefits, I recommend that you use the Contentment Commitment Contract (C3 Form) available on ContentCommitment.com to summarize your commitment and sign it, as you would any other document which legally binds you to the terms. It is, after all, a contract with yourself.

In addition, I recommend that you review this with someone you trust who will support you in your journey, and if possible, sign it in front of them. This makes you feel accountable not only to yourself, but also to this individual who will support you along the way. Lastly, I recommend keeping the contract in a place where you see it regularly - perhaps on a kitchen cupboard, bathroom wall, or anyplace you frequently pass. This will help keep it at the top of your mind until you complete it.

There will be smaller commitments you make along the way, but this is the big one at the end of the process. And while it is the last step, it is one of the most critical ones in the process to ensure that all of the good work you will have done up to that point translates into action and results. I usually try to avoid sports quotes, but the famous (American) football coach Vince Lombardi brings this point home: "Most people fail not because of a lack of desire but because of a lack of commitment."

Your Contentment

It is common for people to fixate on one dimension of Contentment or think of it only in terms of work-life balance, but in order to know where to focus your attention, it is critical for you to think about it holistically. From a chef's perspective, it is vital to balance efforts across the whole of the eating experience, not just one aspect of it. The ingredients of the Contentment Commitment are available to everyone, and now it's your turn to combine them in a unique way that creates the perfect "dish" for you.

◆◆◆

"This is Top Chef, not Top Scallop."
--Fabio Viviani from *Top Chef*

◆◆◆

Your Commitment

1. Download the R3 Worksheets at **ContentmentCommitment.com/Tools** for use in the next several chapters. You will use them to capture your ratings and rankings as you reflect on each dimension and the sub-dimensions within them. You can also use them to capture potential actions that will improve your satisfaction in each.
2. We will be asking questions which will force you to dive deep into each dimension and their subdimensions, and we will explain what exactly is included in each. It is *easiest* and *best* to have the R3 Worksheets with you as you are reading the following chapters, so please take 3 minutes to go to **ContentmentCommitment.com/Tools** now and download them. This will help ensure you capture all the great ideas you'll be generating. Yes, this instruction is the same as #1, but that's because I *really* want you to do it.

CHAPTER 5

The Big Bang Theory
SELF DIMENSION OF CONTENTMENT

THE BIG BANG THEORY

I have a personal connection to *The Big Bang Theory*, as it was my older son's favorite television show for many years, and he may or may not display a few Sheldon-esque qualities. But that's not the only reason this chapter is anchored to this show. If you look at the official description on IMDb, it says it is about "a woman who moves into an apartment across the hall from two brilliant but socially awkward physicists and shows them how little they know about life outside of the laboratory." Hopefully, they had something better for the original pitch as it's not the most exciting description, but it is an example of people so caught up in their professional lives that they appear to be clueless about what else in life might make them happy.

For these reasons, I felt it was a good way to tee up the dimension of Self. To help you think through all the different aspects, we'll work our way through a list of sub-dimensions. I warned you there would be sub-dimensions! For Self, these include Wellness, Professional, Financial, Creative, Cultural, and Spiritual. Think about your past experiences, the present, and what you want to accomplish in the future. Think about things you started but never finished. Think about things you always wanted to try but never did. Just as with the top level dimensions we have introduced, not every sub-dimension will be relevant for every person, so focus on the ones that make sense for you. And lastly, I'm going to call them "Subdies" instead of sub-dimensions because that's what my wife would say because it makes them sound "cute." And because it makes me laugh.

The Subdies of the Self Dimension

After thinking through all the different aspects of each Subdi of Self, you will rate them on a scale of 1 to 10. Remember, a score of 1 is the worst, a score of 10 is the best, and you get to decide what the numbers in between mean for you. As the process gets you focused on how you are feeling about each one, it may stimulate some ideas on actions you could take to feel happier in each area. I recommend you write them down whenever they come to you - you can always review and add more at the end. I'll also share some examples from my personal experiences to try to bring the Subdies to life for you and encourage you to reflect more deeply. Here we go!

CONTENTMENT COMMITMENT

[R3 Worksheet – Self: Wellness, Creative, Professional, Cultural, Financial, Spiritual. Rate First Rate Satisfaction (lowest to highest), Then Rank Importance to Improve (most to least). Three Action lines per category.]

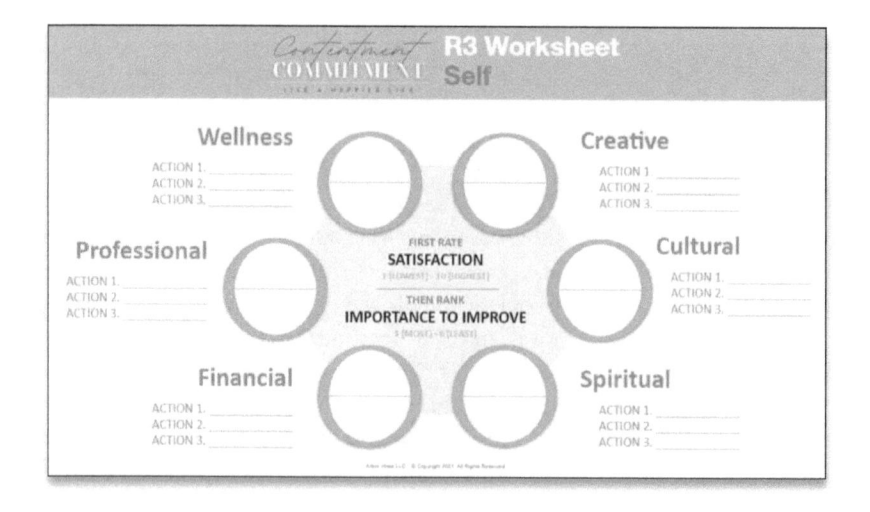

Self: Wellness

The Wellness Subdi of Self includes the most basic of human needs and refers to both Physical and Mental Health. From the Physical Health perspective, probably the most common aspiration is to improve fitness. Nearly everyone seems to have an objective to lose 10 pounds (give or take) and get more toned. Think carefully about your objectives. Are you trying to capture the attention of the entire beach when you reveal your amazing swimsuit body, or are you simply trying to feel comfortable in your clothes without buying a new wardrobe for the heavier version of you? Maybe you just want to be at a weight where you can eat a Popeye's Chicken Sandwich or a Heath Bar Blizzard from Dairy Queen without feeling guilty. Mmmmm Popeye's Chicken Sandwich ... I digress.

With respect to Mental Health, are you happy with your current state, or are you trying to improve it? If you are happy, what do you think is contributing to that feeling? If you're trying to improve, are you focused on trying to manage yourself or do you have a therapist or medication that helps you? Perhaps you have been curious if these options could improve how you feel, but you have been hesitant to prioritize it. What actions could you take that would cause you to rate it higher after they have been completed?

For me, like many people, this has been in and out of focus over time. I struggled the most with physical fitness after the birth of our first child. Despite reading all of the books on what to expect and thinking we were ready, my wife and I had no idea about the immediate and comprehensive effect it would have on all aspects of our lives. Mostly, I just felt too tired to work out, but when I did have energy, it felt selfish to spend the very small amount of free time I had on myself rather than with my new son or my spouse. Some call it sympathy weight, and perhaps that is a way to convince yourself it is a good thing, but for me, I simply don't like the way I look or feel when I am over a certain weight. It wasn't until I committed to prioritizing my physical health that it began to change.

From a mental health perspective, I've not yet had a period in my life where I felt enough stress or anxiety that I felt the need to take medication or meet with a therapist to address it. That having been said, a majority of the people I know have tried one or the other or both at some point, which suggests it is extremely common. And while I believe strongly that the Contentment Commitment can help anyone live a happier life, for those struggling with mental health, it should be viewed as a complement to these options rather than a substitute.

When you have physical energy and positive mental energy, everything you do will be better. As a result, making improvements in this Subdi has an amplifying effect, not only on the other Subdies in the Self dimension, but also on all 6 dimensions of Contentment.

Self: Professional

We can spend the least amount of time focusing on Professional since we already covered this in detail when talking about Personal Engagement. Think about the proportion of time you are giving to this in relation to the other Subdies of Self. Think about how you feel before you start work each day and how you feel when you get home ... or, if you work from home, how you feel when you declare you are done for the day. How would you rate your satisfaction overall? What actions could you take that would make it better?

Would you be happier if you put more of your time into your job or less? If it is more, what are the specific actions you would do more of? If it is less, how exactly might you go about it? Sometimes we may feel stuck in a situation, but there are always options - even if it is choosing to think about the situation from another perspective. While it can be difficult or time-consuming, there are always changes we can make in our professional lives - including changing our employers - which can help enhance our satisfaction.

In my professional career, there have been times when I prioritized having a role which maximized my international travel, times I focused on roles to learn new skills or gain supervisory experience, and times I committed to finding roles in which I could better manage my work life balance. There have also been times when I realized I needed to change employers entirely to surround myself with new people and new challenges. And most recently, this approach helped me realize that anything I spend time on professionally at this stage of my life has to have purpose.

The most important thing to consider in this Subdi is how much of your identity you associate with your career. If you consider each of the 6 dimensions of Contentment include six Subdies, then your professional life is only one of 36 aspects that can impact your happiness. Do you work to live or live to work? If you answered the latter, consider how the satisfaction you get in your professional life impacts your Contentment in the other dimensions.

Self: Financial

Certainly, there are aspects of this Subdi that are tied to the Professional Subdi, since most people's financial health is dependent on the income from their job. However, I have called it out separately because it impacts other aspects of the Self dimension of Contentment as well. The less you have to worry about your financial health, the more your mind is free to explore the other areas which can improve your happiness. Let's break it down into short-term financial health and long-term financial health.

When you think about your short-term financial health, how would you describe it to a friend? What is your confidence that you can pay your bills for the next several months? How does that make you feel? What is your confidence you will have enough money to regularly do things you enjoy? How does that make you feel? What is your confidence you will have enough money for a large purchase outside your normal expenses, such as furniture, a car, or a new place to live? Is your short-term financial health more a source of comfort or stress?

Now, think about your long-term financial health. When would you like to retire? What would you do in your retirement? How much money do you think you will need? How do you know? What do you think is the right age to start planning? Are you confident in your ability to do it yourself or do you need help? Who would you trust to help you? Do you have a plan? If yes, how confident are you about it? If no, why not? Do your answers make you feel more confident, or do they make you feel more concerned? What are some actions you could take to feel more comfortable and confident in your long-term financial health?

In terms of short-term financial health, I started a budget when I started my first salaried job after college. At first, I just tracked expenses by every possible detailed category to try to understand what I was spending. After several months, I evolved it to consolidate some categories with small amounts or sporadic spending. I knew I had enough money to pay bills, but I did not know if I had enough for some of the larger purchases I wanted to make, so I started a savings account and set targets to save for the purchases. Eventually, I incorporated the expected income from my paychecks and started to forecast both my income and expenses. I realized that if I could do this confidently for 6-12 months out, then I knew exactly when I would be able to make the purchases, which made me happy.

There were some aspects of long-term financial health that I started early. For example, I saved the maximum amount possible into a retirement account from the very first paycheck I ever received. Of course, I had no retirement plan at age 22, but I figured if I never had the money to spend in the first place, I wouldn't know the difference. I also started saving for my kids' college tuition when I got married, before either of them were ever born.

There were other aspects of long-term financial health I started much later. I never paid much attention to how the money I saved from my paychecks into retirement accounts was performing. It wasn't until my late 30s that I started to calculate how different things could be with better rates of return. I spent a few years using Motley Fool to try to better understand different investment approaches, and I eventually started investing on my own. The performance of these investments played a big role in my ability to retire at age 47 and it made me wish I had started sooner. It wasn't until I was 40 that I actually made my first version of a retirement plan, and I also wish I had done that sooner.

The point of sharing this detail is not to suggest that this is how anyone else should manage their finances; rather, it is to share enough information to ensure that you are thinking about your approach at a similar level of detail. It is also to suggest that it is never too early to put a plan in place. You can always make changes to it, but without a plan, how can you confidently answer the questions that were posed? There are many different ways to manage your finances successfully, but you have to do *something* to have confidence.

Whatever your approach, the more you are in control, the more you have time and money to explore other things that make you happy. Just like the Wellness Subdi, this is an amplifier for other Subdies and dimensions of Contentment.

CONTENTMENT COMMITMENT

Self: Creative

Let's move on to the Creative Subdi of Self. This is a very broad category which can include almost anything, but common examples include music, writing, poetry, photography, crafts, painting, singing, acting, dancing, and cooking. You have most likely tried one or more of these during your life and enjoyed the experience. And you most likely have tried one or more that you hated too. What these activities have in common is that they all allow us to express a feeling or message in a way that is personally meaningful to us and produce a tangible output that we can share with others.

They are also all actions we take to stimulate our minds and learn new things simply for the pleasure it provides rather than for the purpose of driving a specific outcome. For example, you may want to pursue an academic degree or finish one you started because it gives you a sense of accomplishment. This is different from completing a degree to help you get a higher paying job because it is for pleasure more than purpose. Other examples include learning a foreign language, taking a hip hop dance class, reading a book about the plants and animals native to your area, or watching a documentary on climate change. People are naturally curious but often don't prioritize exploring their curiosities unless it is for a purpose.

Are any of these examples things that you have never explored but are curious to try? Are any of them things you have tried and would like to explore more, but you haven't prioritized? Perhaps you have a hidden or forgotten talent that has the potential to push your life in a whole new direction. Perhaps you need to try a few to see if you are passionate about any of them or help you see that they are not so important to you. Think about all the times someone asked you a question and your response was "I don't know." Think about all the times you asked yourself "I wonder how that works?" Think about the times you wish you had more knowledge about a person, place, or event. What would you explore purely for your pleasure?

Reflecting on my own experience, in every personality test I have ever taken, I come out with the label "Analytical" or a similar variation. While I definitely prefer things to be structured and organized, and it helps me to have a process or framework to address challenges in a logical way, sometimes I like to just plow forward without a script. The Creative Subdi might actually be my favorite one in Self.

When I started making music with my brother in my late 30s, I had never written, arranged or produced a song, never played an instrument, and no one had ever accused me of being a good vocalist. My brother would be quick to tell you I knew nothing about chord progressions or musical theory that would allow me to share my ideas with someone who does. Still, I have found joy in making music because it is something I can create and share with others that is unique and personal to me. And it's a great excuse to get together with my brother.

When I was a teenager, I discovered that I like dancing, but it is not something I get to do much in my adult life, and there reaches a point where it is no longer socially acceptable in the same way ... which unfortunately, I learned on a business trip at a nightclub in Paris sometime in the late 2000s. That was the moment I realized I was "too old to be young, too young to be old." In other words, I still *wanted* to be there, but I realized it was probably no longer *appropriate* for me to be there. I was no longer able to blend in, which made me feel awkward and want to leave. So now, I will sometimes hook up a disco ball, put on some 90s R&B, and dance in my basement until I am all sweaty or injure myself. I don't know why this makes me happy, but as long as it does, I will keep doing it.

For most of my adult life, I have focused most of my learning on skills that would enable me to be more effective at work or to be a better parent. While these are useful, they were definitely more for purpose than pleasure. It has only been more recently that I have started exploring areas purely for pleasure. In the past year, I have learned how to create walking trails through the woods, how to use the Google Translate app to have a conversation with someone in a foreign language (it's pretty cool if you haven't tried it!), and how to get the most distance on a frisbee golf throw. Unless you live in a forest, are traveling to another country, or are training for the professional frisbee golf tour, it would be hard to argue that these are for purpose. While they may seem random, each one of the experiences brought me joy in a different way.

If you had the time, what are a few actions you could take that would improve your rating?

Self: Cultural

I included Cultural as a Subdi of Self because I believe it is a critical aspect for everyone to explore. While the initial association for many are items in the categories of arts and entertainment, travel can be a huge source of happiness too. I realize not everyone has the desire or the means to be a global traveler, but there are plenty of interesting experiences to be had by exploring other areas in your own state, province, or country as well.

CONTENTMENT COMMITMENT

What is so important about travel? Well, travel is how we are exposed to different ideas and approaches, different food and drink, different climates, different priorities and ways of living. It exposes you to the possibility that there may be places in the world where you feel happier and more connected than where you grew up or where you live today. Travel can be local, regional, national, or global, and the farther you work through the list, the more differences you are exposed to, and the more opportunity you have to discover something you never knew you would enjoy.

Is your travel limited to the same destinations every year? Is it providing the same level of satisfaction year after year? How many states or provinces have you visited? How many countries have you visited? If you could choose only 3 places that you could visit for the rest of your life, what would you choose?

Of course, arts and entertainment also offer many ways to get exposed to things you never knew you would enjoy, such as art, music, theatre, and sports. Have you ever attended an opera, a musical, a play, or a concert? Have you ever visited the museums near where you live? If you could only explore one, which interests you the most?

I am fortunate to have attended many musicals and concerts, as well as a few plays. I have never experienced an opera, so I will likely try it eventually, but I am more drawn to the architecture of a grand historic opera house than the performance itself. However, what I am most passionate about in this Subdi is undoubtedly travel. My parents were both teachers so every summer we would embark on weeks-long vacations across the country. I am thankful that I have visited 49 of 50 states (damn you, Alaska!), and I am certain that this planted the travel bug in me early ... though I am equally certain that it is the genesis of a love-hate relationship with trailers, tents, and campgrounds.

Foreign study was a massive part of my experience in college, and I knew before I started working that I would want a job in which I could continue to travel the world. I have visited nearly 50 countries for business or pleasure, and it continues to make me happy. The best is when I can visit with friends and former colleagues who live in other countries. It is also a passion shared by my wife, so I expect we'll continue exploring new places for the rest of our lives, or until such time as we are no longer physically able to do it.

How would you rate your satisfaction in this Subdi?

Self: Spiritual

The final Subdi of Self is Spiritual. This is most commonly associated with religion, but it can also be a philosophy or approach to living that focuses on a connection to something more omnipotent and greater than ourselves. If something helps you clarify your purpose or makes you feel more whole, it is likely to improve your overall Contentment. This is an interesting one in that it is more commonly ranked at the top or the bottom, but it is rarely ranked in between.

Are your thoughts and beliefs based on what you were taught as a child or have they evolved over time? Do you find this is increasingly or decreasingly important in your life? Why? When you think about the spiritual experiences you have had, how does it make you feel? What are actions that you could take that would improve your satisfaction in the Spiritual Subdi of Self?

Of all the Subdies of Self, this is the area I have explored the least. Despite being raised a Catholic and officially Baptised and Confirmed, once I was old enough to decide for myself, I felt there were more teachings and "rules" that I disagreed with than I agreed with, which led me away from the church. Much like physical health, I have observed in others that spirituality and religion seem to come in and out of focus at different times in people's lives for different reasons.

There are some parallels with the Subdi of Worship in the Community dimension of Contentment (which we will get to later), but the main difference is that the Spiritual Subdi is more personal to you and less about being connected to other people. It's about trying to understand your place in the world in relation to the world itself.

If this is a dimension of Contentment you have never explored, you may want to consider experimenting a bit to see if it is something that brings you happiness through a greater sense of peace, understanding, or purpose. Whether it is reading a book, watching a show, or asking friends who have already experimented, there are many ways to expose yourself to different ideas and philosophies.

CONTENTMENT COMMITMENT

Your Contentment

If all of this makes you feel like there is so much more you want to do and explore than you have time for, that is a good thing. You just have to remind yourself that living a happier life is a marathon, not a sprint. If you prioritize one or two actions at any given time, you are always trying something new, satisfying your curiosity, and creating opportunities to discover a new passion. And ultimately, you will feel happier in the Self dimension.

◆◆◆

"I'm not crazy. My mother had me tested."
-- Sheldon Cooper from *The Big Bang Theory*

◆◆◆

Your Commitment

1. If you haven't already, download the R3 Worksheets at **ContentmentCommitment.com/Tools** and pull out the one focused on the *Self* dimension of Contentment.
2. Now that you have reflected on each of the Subdies in the *Self* dimension of Contentment, write down your ratings, rankings, and potential actions that will improve your satisfaction in each.

CHAPTER 6

Sex and the City
PARTNER DIMENSION OF CONTENTMENT

CONTENTMENT COMMITMENT

I wish I could get Carrie Bradshaw to write the intro for this section and then solicit commentary from her friends Samantha, Charlotte, and Miranda. I'm sure Samantha would find a good way to work in something overtly sexual, leaving us simultaneously shocked and curious. But since they are not available (or real), I will channel their spirits. For anyone who is unfamiliar with the long-running show, it chronicles the mating habits of single New Yorkers through the lens of this eclectic group of female friends. I chose this show because it illustrates how different approaches to this dimension of Contentment can make us happier at different times in our lives.

In our younger years, there may be a desire to sample as many different types of partners as possible to better understand which qualities are most important in a potential mate, or simply to enjoy the experience and remain unattached. Eventually, we may choose to live with a partner to see if it strengthens or weakens the relationship. And when we're with someone long enough, there are inevitable questions from family and friends if this person is "the one" or if we will get married. The question of if, when, and why to marry is one of the biggest many will face in their lives.

For those who already have a long-term partner (married or not), the focus shifts more to how to keep the relationship strong while navigating the more mundane aspects of sharing a life together. Everything I've observed in my experience suggests that the keys to happiness are the same, regardless of how an individual identifies, how their partner identifies, or whether the union is considered official or not.

For those of you who are single, casually dating, asexual, polyamorous, or not seeking a partner, you may be wondering, "Should I skip this chapter or read it anyway?" My answer is yes. What I mean by that is, depending on your situation, there may be value in reading it anyway and there may not. For example, if you aspire to have a partner in the future, there is some useful information to consider. If you are actively avoiding taking on a partner, then it will be less relevant. I recommend reading it, but if you start and the examples aren't resonating, then move on to the next dimension.

SEX AND THE CITY

The Subdies of the Partner Dimension

When we introduce a new dimension of Contentment, there are new sub-dimensions, and you know what that means ... yes, more Subdies to rate and rank! After working your way through the Subdies of Partner, you will rate your satisfaction in each on a scale of 1 to 10. Remember, a score of 1 is the worst, a score of 10 is the best, and you get to decide what the numbers in between mean for you. As you have ideas about actions you can take in each area, write them down. Vamos!

Partner: Dating

This Subdi refers to the experiences we share one on one with our partners. These experiences can range from very simple to very elaborate, but they serve as a reminder that spending time together is a priority and a source of happiness. For better or for worse, this most commonly seems to include eating/drinking or entertainment, but of course, it can be anything that the two of you enjoy. Some get the most pleasure out of exercising as a couple or trying new things together. Others get the most satisfaction out of traveling adventures. It doesn't really matter what "it" is, as long as you're doing it together and you are both getting pleasure from it.

Think about the experiences you have enjoyed the most with your partner in the past. Think about what you're missing the most in the present. Think about things you are curious to explore in the future, or things you have talked about doing but haven't prioritized yet.

What do you enjoy most among breakfast dates, lunch dates, and dinner dates? What does your partner enjoy most? Do you prefer meeting up for coffee or having a cocktail at happy hour? Is one easier to squeeze into your schedules than another? What types of coffee houses or bars do you prefer? What kind does your partner prefer?

Do you prefer to go to movies, sporting events, or cultural events? What types of movies do you enjoy and which theatre do you prefer? What sporting events do you like the most? Do you prefer professional, university, high school or other youth sports? What types of cultural events do you like most? Movies, Plays, Musicals, Concerts, Opera, Museums? All of them? None of them? Do you prefer professional, amateur, or youth productions? Are there sporting or cultural events you have never experienced with your partner, but you'd like to? Now try to answer the same questions from your partner's perspective. What does he or she like best? Of the events you have attended, is the balance skewed more towards your preferences or those of your partner?

Is exercising or working out an important part of your life? Is it an important part of your partner's life? Do you exercise together or separately? Why? Many individuals like their own routines and resist bringing a partner into something they consider to be more aligned to the Self dimension. Others find that walking, jogging, or biking together creates an opportunity for uninterrupted conversation (no devices!).

What about traveling? Is this something that makes you happy? Is it something that makes your partner happy? Do you more often travel together or separately? Some individuals have mainly traveled with friends or family and worry that they have to give that up to travel with their partner instead. What types of places do you like to visit? What types of places does your partner like to visit? Are you ensuring that both of your preferences are being considered?

Across all of these examples, there is also an overarching question: do you want *more* Dating or *less* Dating with your partner? If one of you feels you are not doing enough Dating activities together, and the other feels exhausted from all of them, the action might be more about the frequency than the type of activity.

In my own experience, I was most guilty of letting this Subdi slip during the period of time we had two young children and I was working long hours. 30 minutes of mind-numbing television followed by a solid sleep sounded more appealing than finding a babysitter, getting dressed up and going out, costing us both money and sleep. As much as this is understandable, it is all too easy to get comfortable and rationalize neglecting it.

When I reflected on my happiness during this period, I felt decent about the kind of parent I was (or at least was trying to be), but I felt like I was not being the kind of husband I wanted to be. As I shared this with my wife, we came up with some simple ways to improve the situation, which were a good fit for our reality at that time.

One of them was taking a bath together at the end of the day. Up to that point, I had taken very few baths in my life by choice, as it just seemed like a less efficient way of getting clean compared to taking a shower. And even if I had tried, I'm certain there would not have been any scented candles or bath bubbles in the mix. I guess I am a typical man in that these things simply did not occur to me. Much to my surprise, it turns out that a bath is an excellent way to relax and decompress at the end of the day after the kids have finally fallen asleep. And it became the only reliable time of day when I could talk to my partner uninterrupted by kids or devices. Bonus: it costs nothing except for those candles and bath bubbles.

Another example I often highlight from my own experience is the concept of a "lunch date." I have shared this with many friends and colleagues over the years, and often, the initial reaction is that it is ridiculous. But then, almost without exception, those who try it tell me it has become a coveted part of their week. It's super simple: you schedule a day and time to meet for lunch with your partner and honor the commitment like you would any work meeting on your calendar. For us, it was easier than going out at night, since it didn't require a babysitter when our kids were in school. It only required that we both prioritize spending the time going out to lunch together vs. other things competing for our attention during the day. Bonus: lunch menus are typically less expensive and served more quickly.

My wife and I have dabbled in all of the examples I shared above. Sometimes they have been hugely successful and fun and we continue to do it more - travel is probably the most noteworthy of these. Other times, we learn that some activities are more fun on our own or shared with friends who enjoy it more than our partner. For example, my wife tends to enjoy going to concerts with friends more often than concerts with me, and once we both learned and acknowledged that fact, now neither of us feel guilty when she goes to one without me.

Small actions can be as much or more impactful on Contentment in this Subdi than expensive events and gifts. I encourage you to think across the full spectrum as you identify actions you can take that would improve your happiness in this Subdi.

Partner: Intimacy

This would be the perfect place to insert a comment about sex from Samantha. And as someone who was exposed to *Beavis and Butthead* growing up, unfortunately, my brain immediately reverts to "Huh huh huh ... he said *insert*." Sorry, just letting you know there is a lot of useless stuff stuck in my brain along with the useful stuff.

It's important to highlight that Intimacy refers to more than just sex. This can be manifested in hugs, kisses, cuddling, or anything that brings your bodies close together. In addition, emotional intimacy, or feeling a connection with your partner, can be more important and powerful for some than any form of physical intimacy.

How often do you like to be hugged? Kissed? If it was up to you only, how often would you have sex with your partner? Are you adventurous, or do you prefer to stick to the basics? Do you like to cuddle on the couch or in bed, or do you feel like your space is being invaded? Do you prefer to take baths with your partner, alone, or not at all? How connected do you feel to your partner emotionally? How would your partner answer these questions?

I randomly read an article one day that summarized a study which found that people who receive a hug every morning were more productive at school and work than those who did not. The knowledge that my wife wants hugs, kisses, and snuggling much more than I do became a catalyst to start hugging her every morning, just in case. And I started doing the same with my kids for good measure. Undoubtedly, if there was an Analytics team tracking my Hugs Per Week stats, they would have observed a massive uptick because it is not something I ever would have thought to do without prompting. It was a simple action and we joked about it, but there is no question my wife is happier receiving a minimum of one hug per day than she is going days without one.

What are some simple actions you could take to improve your satisfaction? How do you think your partner would answer? What if you just asked them?

Partner: Responsibilities

This is the very definition of mundane. Bo-ring. I'm talking about taking out the garbage, cleaning the bathrooms, doing the dishes, vacuuming - all the fun stuff. The reason it is included as a Subdi is because it has great potential to be a source of conflict with your partner if you do not talk about the distribution of labor.

Do you ever feel like you are doing more of the tasks than your partner? Or do you perhaps feel that you are stuck with the most difficult or gross responsibilities while your partner gets the easy ones? I have seen so many examples where one person thinks that there is an unspoken agreement or understanding about who does certain chores, and their partner is completely unaware and unsupportive of the nonexistent agreement.

As an example, maybe your partner does the dishes most nights and you think you're being helpful by doing them one night. You might be expecting a big thank you, but instead, it leads to an argument with your partner about how little you contribute to doing the dishes and how you are not showing enough appreciation to them the other six nights of the week that they are doing it. Then, you're annoyed because you wonder if you would have been better off not doing them at all. Interesting ...

This Subdi of Partner is amplified if you are living together. And it only gets more amplified when you bring pets or children into the mix. Who is walking the dog? Who is changing the litter? Who is getting up at 2 a.m. to change the diaper? Who is in charge of feeding the kids? Who is driving them to their activities? You get the idea.

One example stands out most clearly from my personal experience. My wife and I rarely ever argue, but we found that after we started living together (and *before* we had kids), we were starting to argue frequently about cleaning the house. I was surprised by this since I like to keep things neat and orderly (shocker!), and I felt that I did more than my share of cleaning by keeping everything picked up. I learned that this was excluded from my wife's definition of cleaning, which was all about disinfecting and scrubbing. I didn't mind taking turns doing the work, but I realized we disagreed on how often it needed to be done. I did mind doing the work when it looked like it was already clean and didn't think it needed to be done.

Even though we didn't really have enough money to do it, our solution was to hire someone else to do the cleaning once every two weeks. I realize not everyone has that luxury, but we prioritized it over eating out more or going out more because it completely eliminated what was becoming our primary source of conflict. More than 20 years later, we have plenty of time to clean, but we continue to hire others to do it for the same reasons as when we started.

The more responsibilities you have as a couple, the more important it is to talk about them and ensure that there is a fair distribution of labor. Any system that works for you and your partner is a good system, but the key is to actually discuss and agree on an approach rather than assuming it will work itself out naturally.

Partner: Financial

Coming in a close second in the mundane and bo-ring category: talking about money and finances. At the same time, this seems to often be at the top of the list of topics that create conflict in relationships with a partner. We all come from different households where money was managed differently, so it makes sense that we would have different approaches and philosophies as to how to manage our own. And the longer period of time we have managing our own finances, the harder it becomes to integrate with someone else who has been doing the same.

When you grew up, who was in charge of paying the bills? Was it shared or owned by one person? Were income and expenses shared or did each parent manage their own? Did the approach work well or poorly? If you were in a two parent household, did both parents work or only one … or did one or both work multiple jobs? Did you rely heavily on credit or was everything paid for in cash? How did these experiences influence your own approach?

Now think about the present. Do you know how much your partner makes and how much they spend? Do you know if they have any large savings or large debts? Do you plan to share your money at some point in the future or keep things separate indefinitely? If you do not share your income, how do you share your expenses? What if one of you has saved for a house or retirement and one has not? Would you pay for their share or expect them to pay for yours? How would your partner respond to the same questions?

Recognizing these are unsexy and sometimes uncomfortable topics, they will very likely lead to conflict if you do not align on an approach that works for both of you. For some, this may include detailed spreadsheets with fancy algorithms. For others, it may be an agreement to discuss big purchases over a certain amount or long-term plans only. There is no right or wrong - just a need to discuss and align before it becomes a problem.

In my own experience, my wife and I aligned on an approach where we share all of our income and all of our expenses. Among other things, it made things a lot easier when we were trying to figure out if one or both of us would continue to work after our children were born. I am closest to the details of our finances, but it is important to her that everyone knows she is fully capable of doing it herself if she needed or wanted to. I have also learned we can have a much calmer and more rational discussion about finances if it is accompanied by a glass of wine. If we had met later in life or not wanted kids, we may have chosen a different approach. The point is that we have discussed and aligned on an approach that works for us.

A common example I have observed among other couples is when one person makes a large purchase without consulting their partner (whether they share their money or not), and then the other partner makes a retaliatory large purchase presumably to show their displeasure or assert their equality. This tends to lead to other instances of making decisions without consulting your partner and can create a bitterness about needing to "ask for permission." Or perhaps it is this feeling which leads to the action? Either way, it is disrespectful to your partner when you choose to do something that impacts them without at least soliciting their thoughts about it.

Would you tell them you're taking a new job and moving across the country without soliciting their input? If yes, it's probably time to move on. If not, show them respect by asking for and valuing their opinions on other issues that affect their happiness.

Partner: Parental

Parental in this instance refers to both the two-legged and four-legged kind of parenting. In other words, it includes any kids or pets that you and your partner are caring for together. It does not matter if they are fully or partially yours or how they came to be in your care. It only matters that you and your partner are responsible for how they are being raised. More fundamental is aligning on whether or not to have them in the first place. In some cases, you may not have a choice. In other cases, you may not agree on when or if to parent another living thing together.

For this Subdi, we'll reflect on it from the lens of your relationship with your partner. Later on, we'll also look at it from the lens of your relationship with the people or pets that depend on you.

Let's focus on kids first, for those that have them or are thinking about having them. Who would you want to be the primary caregiver - you or your partner or both? Would one of you be expected to quit your job? If so, who and why? If both of you plan to continue to work, what is your plan for daycare? A relative? A nanny? A day care facility? When your child wakes up crying at 2 a.m., who gets up to deal with it? Who is in charge of feeding them during the day? Who will drive them to their appointments and activities? What level and type of education do you expect for them? How will they be supported financially? Do you feel like you are always being the "bad guy" while your partner always gets to be the "good guy"? What will be your approach to your children's diet and exercise? How do the views of your partner compare with yours?

From the perspective of taking care of pets, how will you divide the responsibilities? Does one of you always walk the dog or do you take turns? Do you think there should be more discipline or less discipline? How often should they be seen by a groomer or veterinarian? If they get sick, will you spend whatever it takes to help them, or is there a limit? Are you aligned with your partner on these answers?

I've had experience parenting both kids and pets with my wife. With our kids, it was similar to all the reading and preparing we did before they were born. We thought we had discussed all the important items, but we quickly realized that was impossible and tried to figure them out together in real time. We learned that if there was a behavior that was important to one of us to reinforce, then we both had to reinforce it, or else it wouldn't happen. This required each of us to ask for the other one's help if there was something important we were trying to influence.

One of the most important lessons we learned was to choose our battles with the kids and make sure we won them. It's not fun for the parents or the kids if the majority of the interactions are "you can't have this" and "stop doing that." But it can be a big source of conflict with your partner if you are not aligned about which battles to fight, so again, it is very important to discuss and agree on the approach.

With our pets (all cats), there were many of the same potential sources of conflict. These felt just as important in the days before we had kids, but seemed less important once we were having the same discussions about our children. For better or for worse, we agreed to focus our energy on the kids, which made things easier for both of us. It was probably better for our pets in that we stopped trying to change their behaviors or discipline them in the way we had previously.

The key aspects are the same as in the Responsibilities Subdi, but this can be an even bigger source of conflict if you're not aligned with your partner. For those thinking about having kids or pets or both for the first time, the more you share your philosophies on parenting, the more likely you are to enjoy the experience together. While it is unnecessary and unrealistic to have everything perfectly sorted, it is important to discuss as much as you can so you know if there are any disconnects that will cause major conflict before it happens. Any system that works for you and your partner is a good system.

Partner: Communication

You may have noticed a recurring theme throughout this Subdi: they all ask "what does your partner think?" Sometimes it's fun to guess, and the better we know someone, the more often we will guess correctly. However, there is no substitute for simply asking them directly and having a discussion about it. And just because you have discussed something once, it doesn't mean that the answer remains the same over time. Feelings change. Opinions change. So it is critical to continue to communicate how you are feeling across the Subdies of Partner as you have more experiences with them.

How often do you and your partner discuss the questions that have been posed in this dimension of Contentment? Are there some you discuss more frequently or less frequently? Why? Where and when do you typically have these types of discussions? Is it relaxing? Fun? Stressful? Uncomfortable? What could you do to create an environment more conducive to these types of discussions? How often do you think you should be having them? And (you knew this one was coming) how would your partner answer those questions?

I rarely gave this much thought at all because I felt like our relationship was in a good place. However, when we had two small children and I began to feel differently, I tried an early version of the Contentment Commitment framework on my own. While I had some success in the Self and Friends dimensions of Contentment, I still felt out of sync with my wife. So the second time I tried it, I reviewed it with her and asked her to try it with me. This was super insightful and had a much greater impact on both of our satisfaction in the Partner dimension. It seems obvious now, but apparently, I needed to have that experience to learn it.

As I mentioned earlier, a relaxing bath at the end of almost every day became our primary time for connecting. We did not analyze and rank all the options, rather, we tried several different approaches and this seemed to be the environment where we both felt most calm and focused on our conversations. Of course, there were other times and places when we might also discuss these types of topics, but we always knew we would have an opportunity at the end of each day to share what was on our minds ... as long as I wasn't traveling for work.

CONTENTMENT COMMITMENT

For heavier topics, we did start to actually schedule time to do it, and we found that they were always better over wine.

As our kids got older and we had more time and fewer distractions, we naturally started to have these types of discussions in other places. Sometimes over coffee in the morning (though this is my wife's least friendly time of day, so I try to avoid that), sometimes over a walk, sometimes over a happy hour or a meal out. The bath at the end of the day is no longer the daily debrief it once was, but just one of many places we have these types of conversations. What once seemed difficult or uncomfortable now feels natural and constructive, if not always a delight.

As you and your partner have new experiences, it is reasonable to expect that some things will go differently than anticipated, and you'll have to figure it out. It is also reasonable to expect that you'll have some successes which should be celebrated. As a result, it becomes most important that you have time built into your schedules to have regular ongoing conversations about them. Naturally, you will not discuss all of the topics all of the time, but you'll focus on the ones that need the most attention. Whether it is over a walk, a drink, a meal, or a bath, I recommend you prioritize creating opportunities for you to discuss regularly and in an environment that you feel relaxed and undistracted.

And I *might* be biased, but I think the Contentment Commitment framework is a great way to gain insight into how your partner feels about things you might not normally or deeply discuss. I encourage you to share your ratings and rankings with them, and ask them to support you in the actions you will take to try to improve your satisfaction. Ask for their inputs or even ask them to complete the ratings and rankings from their point of view to discuss and review together.

Your Contentment

The questions in this section are some of the hardest in the entire process, so if it feels like it's a lot to absorb, that's ok. They're difficult enough to answer for yourself, but even more so when you try to answer for your partner. Think about what is the best environment for you to have an open and ongoing dialogue with your partner. In the same way you may focus on only one or two actions at a time in the Self dimension, I recommend you focus on one or two at a time in the Partner dimension as well. This will help you try different approaches to see what works best, make some progress you can feel good about, and keep you from overwhelming each other.

◆◆◆

"The most exciting, challenging and significant relationship of all is the one you have with yourself. And if you find someone to love the you that you love, well, that's just fabulous."
-- Carrie Bradshaw from *Sex and the City*

◆◆◆

Your Commitment

1. If you haven't already, download the R3 Worksheets at **ContentmentCommitment.com/Tools** and pull out the one focused on the *Partner* dimension of Contentment.
2. Now that you have reflected on each of the Subdies in the *Partner* dimension of Contentment, write down your ratings, rankings, and potential actions that will improve your satisfaction in each.

CHAPTER 7

This Is Us
DEPENDENTS DIMENSION OF CONTENTMENT

THIS IS US

Since I picked one TV Show that was a favorite of my older son, I had to pick one that was a favorite of my younger son too. Fair is fair. Since this show is not as widely popular as some of the others I picked (at least not yet), I'll share a bit of context. According to IMDb, it is "a heartwarming and emotional story about a unique set of triplets, their struggles and their wonderful parents." In my view, it is an intergenerational drama focused around the Pearson triplets and the moments of love, happiness, heartbreak, and growth they experience in their everyday lives. I like it in this context because it explores the emotions from many angles and points of view, and it feels more like real people issues than "beautiful people" issues that are often the focus in other television shows. It's not for those afraid of crying, but if you haven't binged it yet, I encourage you to give it a try.

It is important to highlight why the word Dependents is used for this dimension. It refers to any living thing that depends on you for their health and development ... though I'll focus on people and pets rather than plants. Sorry, plant lovers. From the people perspective, the most obvious group is kids. If you've got 'em, you know they are all-encompassing and could easily occupy 100% of your attention and energy on their own. It doesn't matter if you spawned them or not - as far as I can tell, they require the same support whether they are your kids, step-kids, adopted, or kids of family or friends in your care.

For people without kids, pets often play a similar role in terms of occupying much of their time and attention, so it is absolutely included in this dimension. My sister-in-law (who is a vet) and her husband have 9 animals living in their house, and I can't imagine the feeding, walking and bathing schedules required to manage them all, not to mention playing with them and trying to get them to behave. However, they generally don't have to go to school, be driven to extracurricular activities daily, or get married, so there are some advantages.

I get the sense that people with pets but no kids do not fully appreciate the challenges of raising kids, and people with kids but no pets do not fully appreciate the challenges of caring for pets. Maybe we should look to people who have both for guidance. For the purposes of this topic, I suggest we focus on applying the concepts to our own realities and leave it at that.

Even if you have no children and no pets, there's a good chance you may have an aging parent that requires some level of support and nurturing from you

CONTENTMENT COMMITMENT

- so that is another aspect of the Dependents dimension to consider. Just as with the kids, it may not technically be your parent, but any grandparent or other extended family member that is aging can end up occupying much of your time and energy at different stages of life.

If you have no kids, no pets, and no parents, you have one less dimension to worry about and you can skip this chapter ... but also, you are missing out on a lot, so maybe you can experiment with a pet with a very short life expectancy and move on from there if it brings you joy.

The Subdies of the Dependents Dimension

As you know by now, introducing a new dimension means introducing the related Subdies. For Dependents, these include Providing, Teaching, Playing, Experimenting, Socializing, and Communicating. We'll review these in detail to explain what is included in each, and then ask you to reflect, rate, and rank. We'll ask lots of questions to stimulate your thinking about each Subdi and suggest you write down any potential actions as you go. Let's do it!

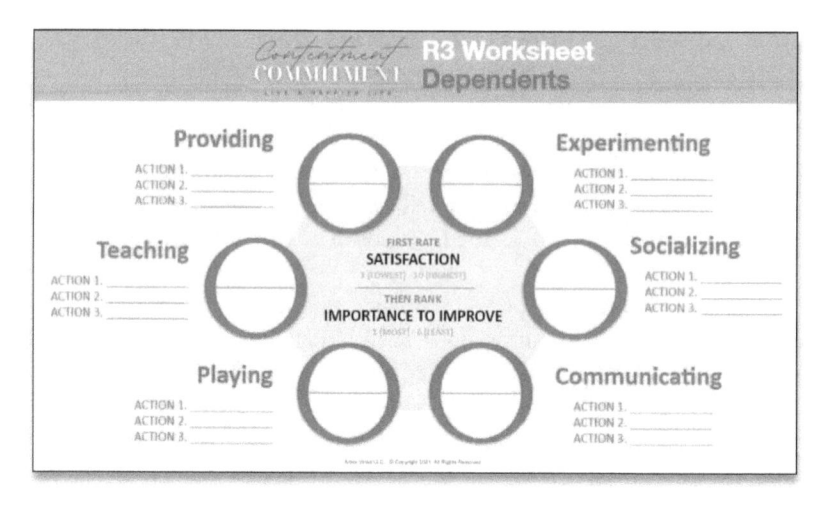

Dependents: Providing

This Subdi includes the most basic and fundamental aspects of Providing for your Dependents. Specifically, it refers to providing food, shelter, and medical care. While this may seem obvious, many people struggle to provide this for themselves, and the responsibility and negative effect on their Contentment is amplified when there is a real or perceived obligation to provide the same for others.

Relative to food, this can range from providing the bare minimum to survive to trying to provide a healthier diet or exposing them to new types of foods. For shelter, this could range from providing them with a roof and temperature-controlled environment to providing more personal space to helping pay for their rent or mortgage. From a medical perspective, it can range from providing basic health care coverage to taking them to appointments or helping pay for medications or premiums.

Do others rely on you for food? Do you have enough to share? Do you feel like more of what you buy is for them, for yourself, or fairly balanced? Do you buy the cheapest option, the best no matter the cost, or somewhere in between? If they are dependent on you financially, what do they do to contribute to the shopping or cooking of food? How would your Dependents answer?

Do others rely on you for shelter? Do you have enough space for them? Do you have enough space for yourself? Are there easy or low cost actions you could take to your existing shelter to make it better? Is moving to a new apartment or home something you can consider? If others rely on you for this, what do they provide in return? If they have no money to contribute, what do they do to earn their keep?

Do others rely on you for medical care? Do they have any other options to receive support? Do you feel it is entirely your burden? Who helps you when you need medical care or support from others? How do you feel about the quality of care? Do you consider medical care for your pets the same as other Dependents or different? What could you do to be more confident about your ability to provide?

I have had extensive experience with kids having helped raise two college-age boys with my wife. I have a few different experiences as a pet owner with both high maintenance and low maintenance cats, but not with any other pets. And I'm fortunate that my parents and in-laws are all still in relatively good health and not dependent on us for food, shelter, or medical care.

With the kids, we were fortunate that we had enough money for food and a house and health care coverage through an employer. So, our challenges were more around trying to get them to eat more than just macaroni and cheese or peanut butter sandwiches, and giving them a reality check when one complained that the other had a bigger or nicer bedroom. To the extent we could influence it, we tried to make sure they had playdates at friend's homes that were smaller (e.g. an apartment where their friend does not have their own room) as well as those that have nicer houses with more space and things. I like to imagine that this helped give them some perspective and be thankful for their own situation, but only time will tell.

With the cats, I was especially frustrated with a cat we picked out from a farm that ended up hating seemingly all humans including us. For the entire time we provided for her, the cat returned amazingly little love and affection and frankly turned me off to wanting any more pets of any kind to avoid being stuck in that situation again. At least she liked the other cat we had at the time. Since my wife felt differently, we eventually adopted another cat, and fortunately, he was much more like a family member, but I'm still a bit scarred.

In my opinion, this is one of the most difficult Subdies to improve because it typically requires more money and/or more time - both of which are usually in short supply. However, I do think there are always opportunities to seek support from others so that the burden does not fall entirely on you, whether it is other family members, friends, neighbors, or social services.

If you could only make one improvement in this area, what would it be?

Dependents: Teaching

While it may seem obvious what would be included in this Subdi, let's think about the sub-Subdies to make sure we're thinking about potential impacts to your happiness from multiple angles. Unfortunately, I am unaware of a "cuter" word for sub-Subdies.

With kids, this may start out with a focus of teaching them to eat, nap, talk, and walk. As they grow, you may focus more on manners and teaching them how to treat their toys and their friends. Once you've moved past the basics, you may want to teach them about a sport or hobby that you love, hoping they will get as much joy from it as you have. And then it shifts to teaching them about how to balance schoolwork, deal with relationships, get a job ... and the list goes on. All of these take time and energy from you, and if you feel you are not doing as much as you can or want to do, this can have a negative impact on your own happiness.

With pets, teaching tends to initially be focused on training them - when to eat, when to sleep, when to exercise. Depending on your approach, you may also teach them which people are friendly and which people are not friendly, and how you want them to act around people in general. Perhaps you want to teach them commands, tricks, or other things that strengthen your connection to them. As they age or you introduce other pets, you may have to teach them some of these things again. How they respond can make you feel successful or unsuccessful as a teacher.

Parents can present an even bigger challenge since they have always been in charge of you, and it is not easy to shift the dynamic to try to be in charge of them for anything. At the same time, it is common to want to be there for them and support them if they did the same for you growing up. Depending on your situation, you may feel responsible for teaching them how to stop doing something they have been doing for years to improve their health, or how to integrate into a new living situation. This is not really referring to teaching them how to use a smart device or stream a video on Amazon Prime, rather, it is helping guide them through major life changes as their ability to do so on their own starts to diminish.

What all of these examples have in common is that they continue to change over time, and just when you think you have mastered something, the next phase comes along and requires more time and more energy.

If you have kids, what are some of the most important things you want to teach them? How do you think you are doing? If you could only teach them one or two life lessons, what is most important to you? How are you doing in those? Who do you know that you think is a great example? What did they do? Would they be willing to share their experiences with you? Most likely, they are proud of some aspects and feel they failed in others, which might give you some comfort in addition to some practical ideas about how to improve.

If you have pets, what are some of the most important things you want to teach them? How do you think you are doing? If you could only teach them one or two things, what is most important to you? How are you doing in those? Who do you know that you think is a great example? What did they do? Would they be willing to share their experiences with you? Aren't these exactly the same questions I just asked you about kids?!

If you are caring for aging parents, what do you think they *need* the most from you? What do you think they *want* the most from you? What is a good balance between the two? What if their doctor gives them advice and they ignore it? What do you view as your role? How would you feel if you were in their position? What do you think is the single most important thing you could do for them?

Coming from a family where both of my parents, my only sibling, and one of my in-laws were all teachers, I feel like a bit of an outcast for choosing a different profession. Still, I've had opportunities to teach with my kids and help coach some of their sports teams.

With our children, I feel like it is a constant state of feeling good about some of the things we are doing and bad about some of the things we are not. For example, when we see our boys getting good grades, displaying good manners, and being good friends, we feel like maybe some of what we've been preaching and demonstrating their entire lives has gotten through.

At the same time, there is guilt that we failed to teach them all the things we wanted to. Neither is conversational in a second language despite several attempts. We failed to show them all of the places in the world we wanted to show them. And somehow, they still either don't see when the trash and recycle are full and need to be emptied, or they simply don't view leaving it for someone else as being disrespectful.

With our cats, I have consistently felt completely incapable of teaching them anything. Despite the fact that one was an adventurous outdoor cat, one was cuddly and mischievous, one was cuddly and lazy, and the other was the angry hater of humans, they seemed united in paying no attention to learning anything we tried to teach them. Hopefully those of you with dogs have had better results.

The most important learning across all aspects is that we can't do all of the things we would like to, so we need to think about what matters most to us and prioritize that. If we accept that it is not realistic to teach our Dependents everything, and if we take the time to think about what is most important and put in the effort to at least get that right, we will always have something to feel good about.

Dependents: Playing

Remember when you spent a large part of your life simply playing? Before adult life moved in and threw play out onto the curb? Those were the days. In this Subdi, we'll think about what playing means in this context when we think about people and pets in your care.

With kids, playing is really simply sitting down on the floor or ground with them and following their lead to spend time doing whatever they want. It could be playing hide and seek, coloring, or pushing miniature trains and cars in circles and making up stories around them. It could be riding bicycles, playing catch, or setting up an obstacle course. It doesn't really matter, as long as you are engaging with them, having fun with them, and making them smile.

While different animals clearly have different needs, playing with pets is just as important as playing with kids for their development and happiness. This might be as simple as throwing a ball, pointing a laser, or taking them to a park. It could be wrestling with them, pulling out a favorite toy, or pulling out a big cardboard box. Again, it is mainly about engaging with them and having fun with them. And while pets don't smile (except for some creepy pet videos I've seen on social media), they have other ways to show us they are happy and having fun.

With parents or other adults in your care, the idea is the same, but the actions will be different. Playing might happen with cards or board games, or watching a favorite show together. For many, it may be more about companionship than anything else, but everyone is happier when another person joins them in an activity they enjoy. We don't lose the need to smile and have fun as adults, we just forget to prioritize it more often with all of the demands on our time.

If you have kids, how often do you play with them? How often do they want you to play with them? What do they like to play with you? What do you like to play with them? What is the balance? When you are playing, do they seem happy? How do you know? How do you feel when you are playing with them? Is it a source of happiness for you or a drain? If you could change one thing about the time you spend together playing, what would it be?

If you have pets, how often do you play with them? How often do they want you to play with them? What do they like to play with you? What do you like to play with them? What is the balance? When you are playing, do they seem happy? How do you know? How do you feel when you are playing with them? Is it a source of happiness for you or a drain? Is every Subdi in the Dependents dimension going to ask the exact same questions about kids and pets?!

If you have aging parents in your care, what activities would you consider as equivalent to playing with them? Do they tend to ask you to join them in those activities, or are you the one who invites them more often? Do they seem to care more about the activity or the time together with you? Do they seem to be enjoying the activities? How do you know? Are you enjoying the activities or is it a drain on you?

When my kids were younger, I prioritized playing with them, and I felt very good about the time I spent with them. Besides building up my knowledge base of Hot Wheels, Thomas The Train, Bakugan, and countless other toys of the moment, I got to see how my boys interacted with things and people. One of my sons was always interested in how things work, and he could assemble and disassemble toys with ease. My other son was more interested in the details and backstory. For example, what exact powers did I think the monster would have? And how would those powers fare in a battle with a different monster?

At the same time, as they grew older, I could see they wanted to play with me less and less. My wife, the social worker, constantly reminded me that this was developmentally appropriate and that it is a good thing that they prefer to play with other kids, but still it made me feel decreasingly useful in this Subdi over time. I also observed that they did not particularly enjoy when playing crossed over into teaching. We could have fun playing soccer or tennis together, but the moment I tried to give them a coaching point, I could see it instantly became less fun for them.

I have fewer personal experiences to share relative to pets, but I expect they would be similar in the sense that they would want to play a lot initially and less over time, and I would need to adapt to be available as much or as little as they needed me. I have not yet had any aging parents in our care, but I expect the inverse may be true with them: they would be more self-sufficient and in their own routines initially but require more companionship and support over time.

These days, I feel my primary role is to occasionally suggest something to our kids that we might play together and always say yes whenever one of them asks me to play something, but I understand that they will engage with me to play less over time and accept that this is probably a good thing overall. I do think there is value in continuing to suggest new things, as frisbee golf has recently become our main group activity and it wasn't even on the list a year ago.

What are one or two actions you could take that would improve your satisfaction in this Subdi?

Dependents: Experimenting

If the word experimenting makes you think of lab rats or drugs, then please reset your mind for this Subdi. Here we are referring to exposing your Dependents to new people, places, and things. I guess when you think of it that way, we are referring to exposing them to new nouns. Since the next Subdi is focused more on socializing with other people, we'll focus on the places and things for this part.

With kids, think of experimenting with places as showing them a park, the beach, or the mountains. Think of it as riding on a bus, a train, and a plane. Think of it as showing them a farm, a city, and a suburb. It could be a movie theatre, water park, or amusement park. Now think about different types of activities: sports, music, art, reading, cooking, movies, TV shows, or video games. Every time you experiment with something new, it is a chance to see if it is something that brings them joy. It is a chance to observe how they react to it, help them get the most out of it, and sometimes to experience something new yourself.

With pets, certainly a subset of the activities above could be the same, but more likely they have to do with exposing them to new foods, new toys, new walking routes, or new places to sleep. The places might be the same, except I haven't seen too many dogs on water slides or roller coasters, but I'm guessing somebody somewhere has done it.

For dependent adults, it can vary from experimenting with new food or restaurants to new technologies that can help them ("Alexa, tell me a joke.") to new ways to exercise. I have heard from many people with dependent adults living with them that it can be more difficult to experiment with them than with the kids, but I'm sure this depends on the people and the living situation.

Whether your focus is kids, pets, or aging adults, the questions to stimulate your thinking are the same. How intentional are you about exposing them to new places and activities? Are these primarily places and activities that you enjoy, or do you select some that are experimental for you, too? In which of the places do they seem most happy? Why? Which activities seem to make them the most happy? How do you know? Do they ask to try new things more often than you have time or money, or do you encourage them to try new things more often than they seem interested in trying them? If you could only take one action to improve your satisfaction in this space, what would you do?

Over time, I have come to refine and simplify what I view as my primary objective as a parent: to help my kids be happy. A critical component of doing that is exposing them to as many different experiences and places as possible, observing how they react, and encouraging them to explore further with the ones that seem to bring them the most joy - whether it is something my wife and I love or not. As a parent, there is nothing better than seeing your kid's face light up doing something they love.

As a lifelong soccer player and lover of the beautiful game, my older son couldn't help but be exposed to soccer, and he played from the time he was 5 until age 12. I thought he was enjoying it (and hopefully he was, to some extent), but it wasn't until I watched him play tennis for the first time and I saw the joy in his face that I realized this is where he should be spending his time. I would have thought I would be sad to see him stop playing soccer, but instead, I felt great that we had helped him find something that brought him so much happiness ... which, in turn, brought the same to us as his parents.

This is similar to the experience of my younger son. He has become very interested in gaming and plays many different video games with many different groups of friends. At first, this frustrated me because I felt he was spending too much time on his devices, and I had my own biases against video games in general. However, it was easy to see and hear him light up when he talked about a tournament he played in, or a close game he just had with a friend, or a group game where they made it past a difficult level - much more so than when he talked about other things. As a result, we shifted our approach to encourage him to explore the world of gaming more and we started to ask him about it more often.

Whatever your angle, if you view your role as helping your Dependents find new things that make them happy, then it will improve your own happiness as well when you succeed. And if you're lucky, they might actually introduce you to something new that you love too.

Dependents: Socializing

Socializing is a fairly general term which can mean different things to different people. For the purposes of this Subdi, we're really talking about all of the same things we discussed in the Playing and Experimenting Subdies, except substituting the "places and things" with "people," and instead of the interaction being with you, it is with others. As with every other Subdi of Dependents, there are some aspects that are very similar across kids, pets, and adults, as well as some that are differentiated.

For people with kids, how often do your children socialize with other kids? When you observe them interacting, what makes you proud and what makes you cringe? How often do you tell them what made you proud and coach them on the things that made you cringe? Is your child always choosing the activity or making the rules? Is your child always following what other kids want to do? Are you happy with the balance? How do they act around friends? How do they act around kids that are not their friends?

How do they socialize with you and other adult family members? Are they more respectful, playful, or fearful? Is it the same with all adult family members, or is it different with different people? Have you observed them interacting with other adults who are not family members, such as teachers, coaches, and neighbors? What do you like and what do you wish was different about the interactions? How is this similar or different to their interactions with adult family members? What about interactions with adults that are strangers?

For those with pets, how does your pet behave with humans that they know? How do they behave with humans that they don't know? How do they behave with other animals? How often do they socialize with each group? What do you like about their behavior and what would you like to change?

For people responsible for aging parents, how often do you interact with them? What is the nature of the interaction? How often do they socialize with people living outside your home? Are you encouraging them to socialize more with you or others? Or are they encouraging others to socialize more with them? How does social interaction affect their mood?

For each of the examples above, what is one action you could take that would have the most positive effect on improving your satisfaction in this Subdi? Among those, which would have the most significant improvement on your happiness overall?

While in and of itself, this seems like a simple and straightforward Subdi, it can have a big domino effect on other aspects of your life which affect your happiness. In my case, it ended up impacting where we raise our children. Before we ever had kids, my wife and I had discussed and agreed that we wanted to live in a neighborhood where our kids could just go outside and play with other kids without everything having to be an arranged playdate. This tended to exist mainly in neighborhoods with lots of cookie-cutter houses built closely together, which is basically the opposite of what we wanted for ourselves.

It also was one of the biggest reasons it was important for me to continue to work from home throughout my career. In addition to playing with our kids myself, I wanted to be able to attend all of their practices, games, concerts, and activities. Those are the places where I get to see them socializing with their friends and observe the dynamics. When they were young, it almost seemed like they had a different personality at school than at home, which probably sounds familiar to anyone who has ever heard feedback at a parent/teacher conference that sounded like the teacher was talking about a different child. As they got older, I could see them developing a more consistent personality and becoming confident enough to show it.

This gave me opportunities to compliment them and (at least attempt to) coach them on different social situations that are common at different ages, and it made me still feel useful as a parent as they needed me less and less. And that made me feel happier.

This is a Subdi many people gloss over, but the more you reflect, the more you realize there are many actions (big and small) that can help improve your satisfaction - especially when you consider kids, pets, and adults that all depend on you and how their needs change over time.

Dependents: Communicating

In the same way that it is critical to communicate effectively with your partner, it is critical to communicate effectively with your Dependents. And arguably, it is a lot more difficult. With kids, the vocabulary is constantly changing. With pets, unless you are a [insert your favorite animal here] whisperer, it is a guessing game. And communicating with aging parents seems to have characteristics of communicating with both kids and pets, though I advise against mentioning that to them. This Subdi is about finding the right methods and moments to give and receive information with the people and pets that depend on you for their care.

For those with children, what do you wish you could communicate to them more effectively? What do you wish they would share with you more often? In what situations do they seem to share more or be in a better place to receive information? Are there times of day they are more open to communicating than others? Do they prefer something formal/structured, or are you able to give/receive more when you keep it casual? Do they want more from you or less from you? How do you know? How can you be more purposeful about creating the ideal conditions regularly to encourage an ongoing dialogue?

For those with pets, what is your primary purpose in communicating with them? Is it transactional or relational? Do you speak to them like you would a human or do you direct them with specific commands? What types of exchanges make you feel like you are a fantastic pet owner that everyone else should emulate? Which ones make you feel the opposite? What can you do to create the ideal conditions for more of the former?

If you have adults in your care, how well do you communicate with them? What do you wish you discussed more and what do you wish you discussed less? In what situations do they seem more likely to give or receive information? In what situations do they stay silent? Do you find yourself treating them like you treat your children or pets? How would they answer that question?

One moment stands out for me in my personal experience with our kids. Before our first son could talk, sometimes he would cry uncontrollably and we could not figure out what he needed. Eventually, we realized there was a 90% chance he was tired, hungry, or needed a diaper change, but even with that, it was often the last one we tried. With our second son, we taught him a few simple hand gestures early on which helped tremendously. I didn't really believe it would work, but much to my surprise, we were able to understand and respond to his needs at that age much more efficiently, which made both my wife and I feel happier as well.

As with most Subdies in this dimension, how you go about this with each of the different types of Dependents changes over time. Just when you think you have something figured out, a new challenge is presented. This can be both frustrating and rewarding, but either way highlights the importance of keeping close to them - in whatever way works best with each individual - to ensure you understand what you need most from them and what they need most from you.

CONTENTMENT COMMITMENT

Your Contentment

Whether you're caring for kids, pets, or parents, there are so many different aspects to manage it's easy to feel like it's too much to handle. And if you have more than one of those, it's even harder. If you focus on the parts that are most important to you *and* that you are in a position to influence, you are more likely to feel happy in the Dependents dimension than if you are going for perfection.

◆◆◆

"We're their parents. We do the best we can. But at the end of the day what happens to them, how they turn out, that's bigger than us."
-- Jack Pearson from *This Is Us*

◆◆◆

Your Commitment

1. If you haven't already (what are you waiting for?), download the R3 Worksheets at **ContentmentCommitment.com/Tools** and pull out the one focused on the *Dependents* dimension of Contentment.
2. Now that you have reflected on each of the Subdies in the *Dependents* dimension of Contentment, write down your ratings, rankings, and potential actions that will improve your satisfaction in each.

CHAPTER 8

Friends
FRIENDS DIMENSION OF CONTENTMENT

CONTENTMENT COMMITMENT

Monica, Rachel, Phoebe, Ross, Chandler, and Joey. If you do not know these names, let me be the first to welcome you to Planet Earth. They are, of course, the characters of the long-running television series *Friends*, which tracks three young women and three young men learning to live and love in New York City. For people of a certain age, you may have had "the Rachel" haircut or sang Phoebe's "Smelly Cat" song or cited quotes from the show. I still use one of Joey's famous lines whenever my wife is looking good: "How you doin'?" Besides the fact that the name of the show is exactly the same as the name of this dimension of Contentment, it also highlights all the joy that old and new friends can bring and how the time we spend with them ebbs and flows as we experience different phases of our lives.

The Subdies of the Friends Dimension

It's a new dimension, so bring on the Subdies! In this case, they include Talking, Visiting, Going Out, Exercising, Traveling, and Changing. I realize it may seem strange to think about different aspects of how you spend time with friends, but I promise it will help you realize how you are attracted to some friends more to discuss work, others to go out partying, others for deep conversations, others to discuss shared interests, and some simply because they have been your friends for so long you're not even sure why you are still friends. The best friends are ones who truly care about you and want to support you in all the different parts of your life and experience them with you.

As you'll be getting used to by now, we'll try to stimulate your thinking around each Subdi of Friends and then ask you to rate it on a scale of 1 to 10. When thinking about your answers to the questions that are posed and others they inspire as you reflect, it is natural to think about actions you could take that might improve your happiness in each one. Collect them as you go and it will be easier to look across the dimension overall in the end. There is no need to come up with 3 actions for every Subdi - it's just a guide and a reminder that there is really no point in coming up with any more than that, since ultimately we will be prioritizing the top few actions across all the dimensions and subdimensions.

FRIENDS

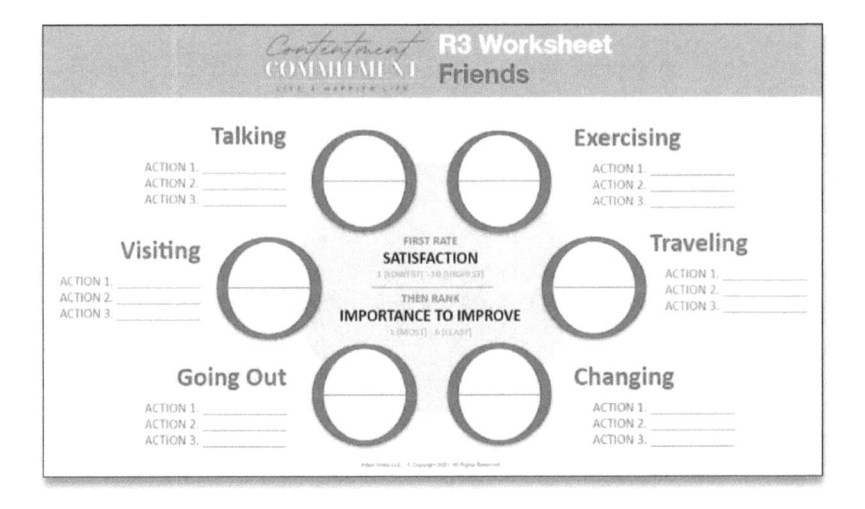

R3 Worksheet — Friends

Contentment
COMMITMENT
Live a Happier Life

Talking
ACTION 1. _____
ACTION 2. _____
ACTION 3. _____

Exercising
ACTION 1. _____
ACTION 2. _____
ACTION 3. _____

Visiting
ACTION 1. _____
ACTION 2. _____
ACTION 3. _____

FIRST RATE
SATISFACTION
1 (LOWEST) - 10 (HIGHEST)

THEN RANK
IMPORTANCE TO IMPROVE
1 (MOST) - 6 (LEAST)

Traveling
ACTION 1. _____
ACTION 2. _____
ACTION 3. _____

Going Out
ACTION 1. _____
ACTION 2. _____
ACTION 3. _____

Changing
ACTION 1. _____
ACTION 2. _____
ACTION 3. _____

Friends: Talking

Some friends are just easy and fun to talk to. Other friends sound like they are disinterested, multi-tasking, or conducting a business meeting with you. Presumably, they have other qualities you value as a friend or you wouldn't be friends in the first place, but talking is not one of them. You may think of this Subdi as simply talking on the phone, but in the event you are living through a global pandemic (you never know, it could happen), talking might happen more via Zoom or FaceTime or Hangouts or whatever your app of choice may be. The point is to focus on conversations when you are not physically together, which tend to focus more on the content of the conversation rather than competing with any other objectives. However you do it, this is the easiest way to maintain a friendship, as it takes the least amount of time and money to simply have a chat.

Which of your friends do you talk to most often? Why? Which do you wish you talked with more often? Why? What do you get out of the discussions that makes you happy? Are your friends good listeners? Do they offer emotional support? Do you listen to their problems and offer them emotional support? Are your conversations balanced, or is one of you always talking and the other is always listening? Do you have friends you wish you talked to less often? After you speak, do you feel energized or drained of energy? Do you feel like the conversations are more for your benefit, their benefit, or mutual benefit? What would your friends say? What changes would you make to get the most satisfaction from talking with your friends?

I have never been a big phone talker personally - whether it is an old school phone call, texting, or video chat. I tend to talk with friends only when there is some type of information being exchanged, like scheduling a trip together or planning an event. For me, the best conversations are ones I have in person with my friends when we are not talking about work or any heavy topics, but instead, we are just relaxing and joking with each other. My favorite people to talk with are the ones that make me laugh the hardest. This is unfathomable to my wife, who talks with her friends daily, weekly, or monthly, depending on the circumstance, and she wants to know about and counsel them on everything happening in their lives. This Subdi would likely be near the bottom of the list for things that could make me happier, but it might be near the top for my wife if she wasn't getting enough of it. How does it rank for you?

Friends: Visiting

Some people prefer visiting with friends more than talking with them. For others, they may prefer to keep the conversation at a distance or limit the conversation to certain aspects of their lives. Sometimes this can be different from friend to friend. And, of course, visiting with friends can mean different things to different people. In this context, it is referring to physically visiting with your friends at their house or at your house. Why call this out separately? Because it is fundamentally different from chatting with them virtually, meeting them out somewhere, or taking a trip together. Visiting someone in their natural habitat is inherently more personal and revealing - especially if there is no clean up in anticipation of the visit.

First, let's think about friends that are relatively easy for you to visit. Perhaps they live nearby or within a short driving distance. Which do you enjoy more: having them over to your house or going to theirs? Why? Are you more relaxed or comfortable in one place than another? Does one of you have kids or pets and the other does not? Is it conversation with your friend or the surroundings (or both) that make visiting enjoyable? What do you usually do when you are together? Do you sit and talk? Do you have tea or coffee? Do you cook together or watch TV together? Is it the conversation with your friend or the activity (or both) that makes visiting enjoyable? After you visit, do you feel energized, or do you feel drained of energy?

Now think about visiting with your friends that live farther away - those which require several hours of driving or a flight for you to see each other in person. Does one of you visit the other more? If so, why? Does one of you have more time and money, does one of you simply make more effort, or does one of you care more about visiting than the other? Does one of you live in a city or town that you both enjoy more? Does one of you live in a nicer place? Is it the time with your friend or the surroundings (or both) that make the visit enjoyable? Is the visit for a specific purpose, such as seeing their new house or new partner or new pet? Or is it purely for pleasure to spend time with each other? Do you feel more happy or less happy after these visits?

Are there friends you want to visit in person more? Why? Are there friends you see more than you need to and you actually want to see less? Why? What would your friends say? How important is this to you or not?

I have learned over time that I like visiting people to see what a day in their life is really like. Don't get me wrong, I also like going out for a nice dinner and bouncing to a few bars acting silly as if we were forever young. But I enjoy it much more if I get to spend some time at their house, talking with their partner or friends, playing with their kids or pets, helping with some mundane task, picking up something from their local grocery with them. This is the less glamorous side of our lives, but it is also the most real part. The other aspect that I have realized is important to me is that the effort to visit is mutual. I have friends I have visited at their homes in 5 different places that never visited me once. At a certain point, I stopped prioritizing seeing them.

What are one or two actions you could take that would make you happier in this Subdi?

Friends: Going Out

Going Out with friends can be casual, like meeting for a coffee or going to a movie. It can be more of an ordeal, like a fancy dinner or an evening of drinking and dancing. It might involve going to a sporting event or cultural event together. The point is that you are physically together and you are doing something outside of your homes. Some people are more social and crave as many of these activities as possible. Others are homebodies and dread being pressured to participate.

How important is this Subdi to you? Do you wish you had more of it or less of it? Maybe some types of going out are enjoyable for you but others are not. Why? Do you enjoy going out for meals but feel like it is setting you back in your health or weight management goals? Do you love dancing but hate being groped on the dance floor or fear someone might be recording it on their phone? Perhaps you have a desire to go out all the time but lack the money. Or perhaps you have money but lack the time or energy. Is it more common for your friends to join you in activities you enjoy, or do you join them in activities they enjoy? Are there "Going Out" activities that you both enjoy equally? Do you ever talk about it with them?

If you could only do one of these activities in a week or a month, which would you choose? If you could pick only one friend to join you, who would you invite? How often do you do that activity currently? And how often do you go out with that friend?

There were times in my life when Going Out with Friends would have been near the top of the list of most important things to keep me happy. In my 20s, I loved visiting as many bars and clubs as possible with different friends in different cities. Even before HGTV existed, I was fascinated by architecture and design that made a place feel hip. I loved when whoever was controlling the music was fully in sync with the vibe of the place and the people in it. And I loved that I was already married and didn't have to judge the success of a night out on whether or not any girls showed interest in me.

And then we had kids. And much to my surprise, all I wanted to do was stare at them and play with them and hang out with other people who were equally fascinated by their own kids or willing to fake it with ours. Going Out became almost entirely focused on family activities, and I didn't really miss Going Out with my friends. Plus, I greatly enjoyed seeing many of my friends go through the same cycle and getting to be a part of it.

Eventually, as our kids spent more time with their friends and were occupied for more hours of the day, we had time to think about Going Out with friends again. We have rediscovered the pleasure, but of course, now it looks very different. A Happy Hour cocktail at one place, an early dinner at another, and a dessert or after-dinner drink somewhere else makes us feel like we've partied all night, but in reality, it has us home and in pajamas by 9 or 10 p.m. We enjoy when our friends join us for some or all of the evening as their schedules allow and it is perfect for us.

What actions could you take that would improve your satisfaction in this Subdi of Friends?

Friends: Exercising

Intentionally or unintentionally, many people tend to have different groups of friends for different activities. For example, there may be some friends that are the most interesting to talk to, but they dislike going out. Others may always be up for going out, but you find they tend to be less interested in anything else. Still, others may fall into the category of friends you primarily exercise with.

FRIENDS

Sometimes this pattern of behavior leads us to spend more or less time with various friends who are activity-dependent based on how much time you spend doing those activities rather than what makes you the most happy. .

I feel like the Exercising Subdi doesn't really need an explanation like some of the others, but to eliminate any doubt, we are talking about activities like walking, doing yoga, or working out with friends. Essentially, it's just another form of Going Out, but it tends to come with more health benefits and less calories. For some, it is really about the conversation or companionship. For others, it is about how they feel during or after a good workout. And for others, it's associating something enjoyable with something they may not consider to be fun on its own.

What type of exercise do you prefer to do with friends? How often do you do that with friends? Do you find yourself doing exercises you prefer to do with friends on your own? Why? Do you find yourself doing exercises you prefer to do on your own with friends? Why? Are you typically the one inviting others to join you, or do you wait for others to invite you? Is it easy to get together or complicated? Is it free or does it cost money? Do you spend more time with some friends when you are focused on your health and less when you are not? Or is it more dependent on when they are focused on their health?

How do you typically feel while you are exercising with friends? How do you feel after? If you could change only one aspect (frequency, people, type of exercise, location, etc.), what change would have the biggest impact on your satisfaction/happiness?

I played competitive soccer for over 40 years of my life, so for a long time, I did not need to do much else outside of that to stay fit. But after college, the fitness aspect became an individual responsibility, and so I began running for the sole purpose of being fit enough to play soccer well. I found when I was traveling and could run in a new location, I enjoyed it because I was distracted by new surroundings. When I ran at home, I began dreading it as it was more difficult to distract myself. Running with a friend made it not only bearable but enjoyable, as good conversation replaced counting strides or minutes until the run was over.

I have had only a few periods in my life when I attempted to lift weights for any sustained period, as you would suspect if you saw my middle aged dad-inspired beach body. However, when I did, I had the opposite experience that I had with running. I found I preferred to squeeze in a workout whenever I could, instead of coordinating with someone else's schedule or trying to time my workout with theirs. The duration tended to be shorter, so it was the conversation that was distracting the workout.

The point is that it may not be as simple as wanting to work out with friends more or less. It depends on the nature of the exercise, and the location, ease of access, cost, timing, and people as well. If you haven't already, I recommend experimenting with different types of exercise with different friends and paying attention to what makes you feel the most happy.

Friends: Traveling

I realize we have touched on traveling in a couple of other areas. In the Self dimension of Contentment, we thought about it as an element of cultural exploration, and in the Visiting Subdi of Friends, we talked about traveling near or far to meet with friends in their homes. For this Subdi, we are talking about traveling with friends or meeting friends in a neutral location. Whether it is with one friend or a group of friends, it is about experiencing something out of the ordinary and having fun together.

Let's think of this in two basic groups: "couples trips," where you and your partner are joined by one or more other couples with whom you are friends, and "guy trips" or "girl trips" that are taken without a partner. Both of them can be super fun, but for those with a partner, there is also a potential source of conflict if the majority of these fun trips are without them. Just as when we discussed travel previously, this does not have to be exotic, expensive, or far away. It could be as simple as renting an AirBnB in a nearby town or city you'd like to explore.

Have you taken any trips with your partner to meet other couples somewhere? What did you like most about it? What did you like the least? Were you the organizer or someone else? What would you do differently next time? If you've never tried it, why not? What "guy trips" or "girl trips" have you taken? Who did you meet? Where did you go? What did you do? What did you like about it and what did you dislike? What would you do differently if you did it again? If you could only go on one trip this year, would you want to go with your partner or on your own? Why? Who would you invite? Why? Where would you want to go? Why?

When you think about your responses to these questions, you may find an unexpected parallel to the Exercising Subdi of Friends. It's likely not as simple as whether you like traveling with friends or you don't, but instead, it depends on the purpose, the location, ease of access, cost, timing, and the other people who are going. What combination of those things is most appealing to you? What is the possibility to take the lead in organizing a trip with those characteristics?

I can imagine that by this point, you must think I over-analyze every action before doing it, but it is really more a matter of reflecting on my experiences. In the same way that paying attention to what types of foods, spices, and drinks you like helps you make better choices when ordering at a restaurant, paying attention to the types of travel experiences with friends that you like can also help you make better choices and get more happiness for your time and money.

In the realm of "couples trips," I have learned over time that I actually prefer to travel with two or more couples rather than just one. This is because people go to bed and wake up at different times, have different levels of energy, and want to do different activities. When there are only four people, groups tend to do everything together, which means you have to negotiate and agree on everything. When there are six or more people, it is common for the group to break up at different times, which allows more of the individuals to spend more of the time doing the things that make them happy.

This is exactly the opposite of my preference for the Going Out Subdi, where I prefer to go out with one couple rather than multiple. This is because we can typically have one conversation we are all a part of rather than splitting into factions or only talking to the person who happens to be sitting next to you. This doesn't mean I dislike when we go out with more than one couple or travel with only one, but I know I am likely to enjoy it more when we do and will try to influence it that way when I can.

The "guy trips" I've enjoyed the most generally have little or no agenda and were with friends just looking for a break from work and their daily lives. While there may be a little time talking about serious topics, it's mostly just joking around, reminiscing, and having new experiences we can laugh about later.

For those with kids, you can also attempt traveling with one or more other families. However, this is the most difficult in my opinion because in addition to the adults going to bed and waking up at different times and wanting to do different activities, you also have kids doing the same. And it is hard enough finding another couple where all four people get on well with each other in any combination, but when you throw kids in the mix, it is nearly impossible. If you are lucky enough to find another family where all of the adults and kids get on well with each other in any combination, hold on to it forever, as it is a rare gem.

Traveling with friends is another example of a Subdi which can have positive effects on other dimensions of Contentment as well. But it also has the potential to have negative effects on other dimensions of Contentment if you have a partner and you're not in sync on the frequency and type of travel, so it's always a good decision to include them in the planning.

Friends: Changing

Some friends have been with you since you were a child. Others were picked up along the way as you took on new jobs or moved to new places. Sometimes you may have been looking to make new friends actively, and other times it may have happened naturally without any effort or intention. And sometimes you can actually be happier by letting go of a friendship that is not mutually beneficial.

These "leftover" friends may always bring out the worst in you, only want to do activities they like, never visit you, or constantly drain your positive energy without giving any back. If you have more things you want to do and try, and more people you want to spend time with than you have time to do it, why would you give away your precious limited free time to people in this group?

The Changing Subdi is not just about letting go of old friends that only care about the old version of you. It is also about adding new friends that are more aligned to the current version of you. As your life has changed, most likely many of your interests have changed, and it makes sense that you would gravitate towards others with shared interests. Especially for those moving to a new city or town, it is very important to make new friends there to feel connected and happy. Whether you join a social group, book club, sports team or community organization, there are many ways to find others outside of your work and your neighborhood.

How do you feel about the people you call friends? Are there some you value more than others? How do these friends support you? Are there some who seem to care more and give more than others? Which friends are from periods of your life when you had different priorities? Which friends are from periods of your life more aligned to your current priorities? How much time do you spend with each? Why? Do you wish you had more friends, less friends, or different friends? What do you think are the most important qualities in a friend? Which of your friends have those qualities?

When I was in high school, I thought it was cool to have as many friends as possible, but in hindsight, for most of my friends back then, I think I was on friendly terms with them rather than actually being friends with them. After a few years in college, there were only a small number of people from high school

FRIENDS

that I actually still considered friends and made an effort to stay in touch with. And as I shared earlier, once I got married, the list of old friends got smaller, and once we had kids, the list of old friends continued to shrink.

Fortunately, we also gained new friends during the same time periods because we felt a connection to people who were going through similar life experiences as us, and we could learn from each other and share with each other. This isn't to say that I stopped enjoying spending time with old friends. On the rare occasions I see them, it is usually enjoyable, but I do not prioritize seeing them because the things we want to do are so different. At first, I felt sad about this and a bit guilty that I wasn't able to be more flexible. Over time, I came to view this filtering as a natural process, and I became more intentional about which friends I spend the most time with.

For me, the best friends are the ones who truly care about me, want to support me in all the different parts of my life as it changes, and enjoy experiencing them with me. Investing most heavily in these relationships is how I get the most satisfaction from this dimension of Contentment. How will you get the most satisfaction?

CONTENTMENT COMMITMENT

Your Contentment

Friends come and go. Sometimes the turnover is healthy and sometimes it hurts. Sometimes it is worth making the effort to sustain a great relationship and sometimes it isn't. What attributes do you value most in a friend? Are you prioritizing your friends with those attributes? When you're able to understand what you give and get in a friendship and compare it to what you value, it becomes easier to know what actions to take to improve your happiness in this dimension.

◆◆◆

"Hi, I'm Chandler. I make jokes when I'm uncomfortable."
-- Chandler Bing from *Friends*

◆◆◆

Your Commitment

1. If you haven't already (and why wouldn't you have by now?), download the R3 Worksheets at **ContentmentCommitment.com/Tools** and pull out the one focused on the *Friends* dimension of Contentment.
2. Now that you have reflected on each of the Subdies in the *Friends* dimension of Contentment, write down your ratings, rankings, and potential actions that will improve your satisfaction in each.

CHAPTER 9

Modern Family
FAMILY DIMENSION OF CONTENTMENT

Here is another one that's a big stretch from the name of the show to the name of the dimension. Sometimes it's ok to be literal or obvious, right? For those unfamiliar with the show, the IMDb storyline describes it as "... an honest, often-hilarious perspective of family life. Parents Phil and Claire yearn for an honest, open relationship with their three kids, but a daughter who is trying to grow up too fast, another who is too smart for her own good, and a rambunctious young son make it challenging. Claire's dad Jay and his Latina wife Gloria are raising two sons together, but people sometimes believe Jay to be Gloria's father. Jay's gay son Mitchell and his partner Cameron have adopted a little Asian girl, completing one big - straight, gay, multicultural, traditional - happy family." Side note: Sofia Vergara (who plays Gloria) is my celebrity crush that I have followed since her days on *Fuera de Serie*, so it feels right to bring her into the discussion somehow.

While not every family will include every aspect of this representative modern family, nearly all can relate to at least some part of it. In the same way, not every Subdi of the Family dimension will be relevant for every person, but we'll cover all the possibilities with grandparents, parents, siblings, aunts and uncles, cousins, and extended family. To differentiate from the Dependents dimension, we'll focus on those family members which are not dependent on you for their care. And while we kept the Subdi names simple, of course it includes all the possible variations on the theme - for example, parents might refer to birth parents, adopted parents, step-parents, or any combination of them or others who played the role of a parent.

The Subdies of the Family Dimension

As usual, I'll pose a bunch of questions to try to stimulate some self-reflection with the objective of helping you rate your satisfaction in each Subdi of Family, and then rank based on what is most important to improve right now. As you do this, you'll likely think of some actions you could take that would improve your satisfaction in each, so please write them down as you think of them, and we can organize your thoughts at the end.

R3 Worksheet: Family

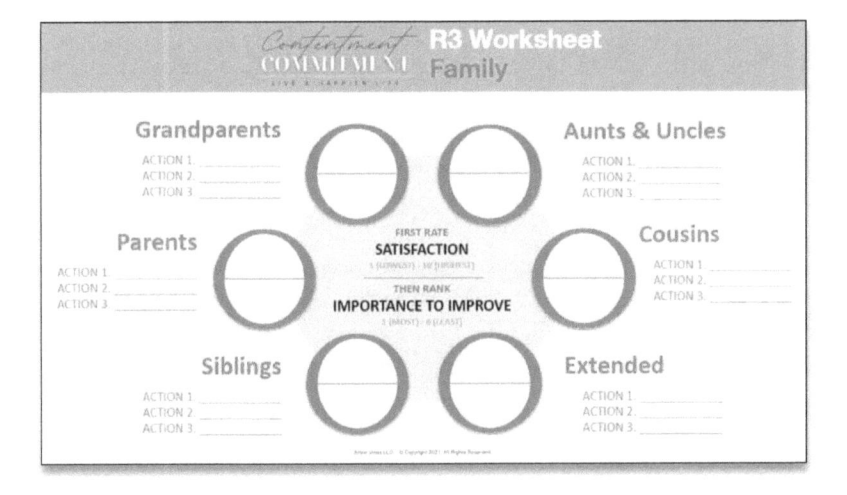

Grandparents	ACTION 1, ACTION 2, ACTION 3
Aunts & Uncles	ACTION 1, ACTION 2, ACTION 3
Parents	ACTION 1, ACTION 2, ACTION 3
Cousins	ACTION 1, ACTION 2, ACTION 3
Siblings	ACTION 1, ACTION 2, ACTION 3
Extended	ACTION 1, ACTION 2, ACTION 3

FIRST RATE SATISFACTION (LOWEST - HIGHEST)
THEN RANK IMPORTANCE TO IMPROVE (MOST - LEAST)

Family: Grandparents

The good news about the Family dimension is that the Subdies are pretty self-explanatory. Hopefully you all know what grandparents are without me mansplaining it to you. The main thing to consider about this Subdi is that the older you are, the less likely it is that your grandparents are still alive. So, if you are lucky enough to have grandparents that are still alive, it may be more important to prioritize spending time with them while you still can.

For those that still have them, how often do you see your grandparents? Do they live near or far away? Do they live alone, with a partner, or in a group setting? What do you enjoy the most about the time you spend with them? What do you enjoy the least? What do they enjoy the most about their time with you? How do you know? How much do you know about their days as kids or young adults? How did they meet each other? What were your parents like as kids? What advice do they have to share?

It's easy to feel guilty that you should be spending more time with your grandparents, but it's important to remember that the happiness you may get from it (and that they may get from it) is as much about quality as it is quantity. And quality time means different things to different people. I have observed grandparents of friends who are quite excited to tell you about events from their younger days, as well as those who prefer to debate politics and religion, and those who simply want someone to play checkers with them without talking at all. I recommend asking them "What do you like to do most?" or "What activity makes you most happy?" and then also let them know what activities you like doing the most with them.

CONTENTMENT COMMITMENT

Unfortunately, all of my grandparents have passed. I knew my maternal grandfather and paternal grandmother but only as a young child, so my time with them was more about my parents' choices than mine. However, my maternal grandmother moved back to Michigan after her husband died to be closer to family, and I got to know her better as a high school and college student. In fact, she came to nearly all of my college soccer games when she lived in town, which I greatly appreciated. And we were able to spend the most time as adults with my paternal grandfather, as he lived about an hour away from us during the time we lived in Florida. I enjoyed that he got to know our older son a bit and we got to learn much more about his life during that period.

In the spirit of the *Modern Family* show, my paternal grandfather also remarried and, after she passed, had a girlfriend ... whatever that means when you are over 80 years old. We viewed them as bonus grandparents despite the fact that we immensely enjoyed our time with one and let's just say "less so" with the other. But they are both part of my grandparent experience. While I didn't always look forward to visits, I was always glad we made the effort. In hindsight, I do wish I had listened more and talked less, and asked them how they wanted to spend the time together.

After I got married, I inherited my wife's two living (paternal) grandparents. They lived well into their 90s and we visited with them frequently at their home on the lake. I think they just loved being surrounded by family and entering into and ducking out of conversations as they pleased. They were always up for a game of cards or a good family board game. Our lives were very busy and it often felt difficult to squeeze in visits, but I'm thankful that my wife prioritized this and I got to be a part of it.

As you think about the time you spend with your grandparents and what actions you could take to get (and give) more happiness from it, I encourage you to think of it in basic terms. The more you both enjoy your time together, the more time you will choose to spend together. When it is enjoyable for both of you, it is more likely to bring you happiness. So be direct and make sure you are getting the most out of whatever time you have left with them. You never know when it will end.

Family: Parents

For many kids, parents are the annoying people who won't stop talking to you, constantly telling you what you can and cannot do, when you have to be home, embarrassing you in front of your friends, and trying to make you do things you don't want to do and eat foods you don't want to eat. They don't even know the cool video games, TV shows, or catch phrases. For some reason, my mind drifts to the classic *DJ Jazzy Jeff and Fresh Prince* (aka Will Smith) hit from the 80s "Parents Just Don't Understand."

But then something happens as we get into our teens - we begin to appreciate some of the things our parents are sharing and start to realize they were actually kids once too. As we become young adults, we start to feel grateful for them even more when we realize some of the things they did for us. From changing our diapers to spoon-feeding and rocking us to sleep in the early years, to playing games, helping us learn to ride a bike and helping with homework in the middle years, or maybe even helping get us our first car or helping pay for college in our later years. I realize everyone's experience is different, so understand these are just examples.

For those of us that go on to become parents ourselves, there is a whole new level of understanding and appreciation. You realize that there is no instruction manual and you do the best you can with the experience, time, and energy that you have at any given moment. You try to incorporate the best of what you've observed in parenting along the way while avoiding the worst parts you said you'd never do. You realize the responsibility that you have, and more than anything, you just want your kids to be happy.

Before you start to reflect on the barrage of questions I will hurl at you, I'll remind you that this is differentiated from the Dependents dimension. If your parents live with you and you are caring for them, that is a very different angle than what we're talking about here. If your parents are alive and not living with you, then this Subdi is meant to help you think about what actions you could take that would make you feel better about the relationship you have with them. Let's reflect.

How often do you see your parents? How often do you talk to them? What do you talk about? Do you enjoy the conversations? What do you do when you're together? What parts of your interactions make you feel good about your relationship? What parts do you dislike? How much do you know about their lives before they were your parents? What influence do they have on your kids (if you have them)? After seeing them or talking with them, do you typically feel happy or unhappy? Why? What can you do about it?

My parents have been hugely supportive of my brother and I throughout our lives. They have done all of the things I listed above and more, and I am grateful to have them. Despite this, in our relationship as adults, I find I do not always love our conversations. This is probably due to the fact I am not much of a phone talker, and they often tend to be transactional ("what do we need to know?") or one-sided. I get detailed updates about people and events I care about very little, and few questions about what's happening in our lives. I wonder if I will do the same when I reach the same age.

One thing I discovered (actually my sister-in-law discovered and shared with me) is a tool called Storyworth. It is most commonly given for Mother's Day, Father's Day or a milestone birthday, but it is basically a massive list of questions for one or both of your parents. You can choose from a list or create your own, but either way, it sends one question per week to them and collects their responses. Some are just a few sentences, others might be a few paragraphs, and they can choose to include photos if they want (assuming your parents can figure out how to upload a photo on the worldwide Internet FaceGoogle thing). After a year of this, the company puts it all together and sends it to them in a printed book. It's a great way to ask questions that might be more difficult to work into your regular conversations and learn more about them. It also makes for good conversation topics when you do speak to get out of the rut of the regular exchange. If you haven't seen it, I highly recommend it.

Once I was married, I gained another set of parents with my mother-in-law and father-in-law. While they obviously didn't raise me, they have shown the same amazing support for their daughter and I that my parents have shown, and I feel lucky to have them as well. They also have their own idiosyncrasies, of course, but I tend to speak with them only when we visit in person. Since we speak less regularly, I do not have the issues I highlighted with my parents, but I also feel like I probably don't know them as well as I could or perhaps should.

I believe that the more you both enjoy your time together, the more time you will choose to spend together. And when it is enjoyable for both of you, it is more likely to bring you happiness. At the same time, I am often reminded by others who have lost their parents that I should value time together regardless of the quality. As a result, I have stopped trying to redirect our conversations and get frustrated about aspects of them, and instead try to follow their lead and be thankful for the time. Many don't have it and you never know when it will end.

Family: Siblings

If you have any, you know your siblings are the only ones who can truly understand what it was like to grow up in your house with your parents, for better or for worse. Your brothers and sisters are the ones with whom you shared childhood experiences that shape much of how you view Contentment (and everything else) today. I have encountered people who are not on speaking terms with their siblings for long periods of time, people who have lost a sibling, and people who live on the same block as their brother or sister. Whatever your situation, they are always going to be your siblings, no matter where they are or what your relationship is.

How many siblings do you have? Brothers or sisters? How often do you speak with them? How often do you visit with them? What kind of relationship do you have with them? Why? What kind of relationship do you want with them? What are your favorite activities to do together with them? What do you enjoy the least? If you have kids, what influence do your siblings have on them? How do they make you feel after you speak with them or spend time with them?

I have one older brother, who takes every chance he can to ask other people who they think is the younger brother. It's a no-lose proposition for him, and he has more hair than me, so he often gets the nod. As kids, our three year age difference was just close enough that we could do a lot of activities together, but also just far enough apart that I became uncool as my brother was a teenager. Fortunately, early in our adult lives, we started hanging out and having fun together in a variety of ways. For the past 10 years or so, we have connected in a new way - making music together. He provides the musical abilities on keys and guitar, and I have developed my skills with lyrics, vocals, arrangements, production, mastering, publishing, and marketing. These are mostly the parts my brother does not enjoy, so it's a good partnership. We have released 9 albums under the artist name *T Street Players*. We don't take ourselves too seriously, but we do take pride in what we create, so check it out if you're curious. If nothing else, it's been a great excuse to get together more often.

Just over 10 years ago, my brother introduced us to his long-term girlfriend, and eventually, they married. She is a great example of someone who is family before they are officially family. Despite tragedy and drama in her own life, going to school to change professions, and finding her way in her new job, she has consistently prioritized being a part of our family - including regularly visiting, spending time with our kids, and talking with our parents.

When I got married, I also gained a sister-in-law and eventually a brother-in-law (or whatever it's called when your sister-in-law gets married). There have been times I have seen them frequently and times we have gone long periods without seeing them much at all. I am thankful that our kids got to spend lots of time with them when they were younger, but also wish we lived closer together and had more activities which we all enjoyed doing together.

Assuming your siblings are relatively close to you in age, it is reasonable to expect you have more time to work on these relationships, but there is no guarantee. What if the next time you see them was the last time you saw them? What would you want to say? How would you want to spend the time? How would they answer those questions? Whether separated by philosophies, values, or physical distances, I recommend you keep trying until you find something that keeps you connected. Even if the relationship feels one-sided for an extended period, they are likely to reciprocate eventually.

How do you rate your satisfaction with your relationship with your siblings?

Family: Aunts & Uncles

Who knew that your parents could have brothers and sisters too? It's funny how when you're a kid, you don't even realize why you have aunts and uncles or who they are. They're just relatives you likely see more often than most others. Sometimes you get people that are like aunts and uncles without actually being related to you. If you have that, I recommend making sure you know who they are and why they are there. You may also have people who are technically great aunts and uncles, but functionally seem more like your aunts and uncles. If you don't have any of these, I'll see you in the next Subdi.

How many aunts and uncles do you have? How often do you talk with them? What do you talk about? Do you ever ask them about growing up with your parents? What dirt do they have on your parents? Do you enjoy the conversations? How often do you see them? Why? What do you do when you are together? Is it fun? What influence do they have on your kids (if you have them)? Do they have kids? Does that make it easier or harder for you to spend time with them? How do you feel after visiting with them? Do you wish you spent more time with them, less time, or just used the time you have differently?

My dad has one sister and my mom has one sister, so I grew up with two sets of aunts and uncles. One pair lives in a small town in upstate New York where my dad grew up. We used to see them a lot when I was young, probably because they had kids that were of a similar age to my brother and I and because we had many other relatives in the area. The other pair lived in the Pacific Northwest and had kids that were quite a bit younger than my brother and I. We saw them significantly less, presumably due to the distance and because it was not as easy for the kids to occupy each other while the adults hung out.

In my early adult life, we still saw my aunt and uncles in New York with some regularity, mainly because we stayed in touch with our cousins who lived in the same area. However, as our cousins had children of their own and so did we, we began to see them less and less. As a result, we saw my aunts and uncles less and less. They used to make trips to visit my parents in Kalamazoo, and I would always make sure I go to see them there, but these have decreased over time too.

During the same period, I saw very little of my aunt and uncle on the west coast. I'm sure the combination of me working full time, the age of their kids, and the fact that they were going through a divorce all were factors. Nevertheless, I just didn't see them as much, and therefore, I didn't get to know them as well. My aunt would visit my parents in Kalamazoo from time to time so I was able to see her there, and I also made a couple of trips to visit her and my cousins.

What I do know about my aunts and uncles collectively suggests they are all very interesting people. Two are dairy farmers who pretended to purchase a sheep for us for a wedding present, and two lived together in a commune in the 70s. I am certain they have many interesting stories from their younger days and much to share about my parents as well. I have enjoyed the time I have spent with them as an adult, and wish I saw them more frequently.

After getting married, I inherited many more aunts and uncles through my wife's family which is much larger than mine. While there are many interesting characters in that group as well, it also makes it even more difficult to spend time with my side of the family. I mainly feel guilty that I have so little time with them, but I also feel guilty that I really only want to spend time with some of them.

Based on my own experiences and observing others, these relationships seem to be more prominent when you're young and then less so as you grow into an adult. Much like the examples in the Friends Subdi, it is not necessarily because you value them less, but because of how your lives change. Depending on how similar or different your aunts and uncles are from your parents, it can be super interesting to learn how people with the same upbringing end up in such different places with different lives. It also highlights how much of Contentment is dependent on our own choices compared to our childhood experiences.

If you could make one change in this space to improve your satisfaction, what would it be?

Family: Cousins

I remember when I was in middle school, there was a time when all the kids called each other "cuz," in the same way some guys call each other "bro" even

CONTENTMENT COMMITMENT

though they are not brothers. I don't know why it was a thing, but it seemed like anyone that you liked or thought was cool could be your cuz. Of course, actual cousins (at least first cousins) are the children of your aunts and uncles. Some people have more liberal definitions of a cousin as anyone who is somehow connected to your family that is similar to you in age that you hang out with. I honestly don't even know the definition of second or third cousin or once-removed or any of that, nor do I want to. For the purposes of our discussion, choose whatever definition works best for you.

How many first cousins do you have? How many "other" cousins? Which ones did you hang out with the most as a kid? Why? Which ones do you hang out with the most as an adult? Why? What do you enjoy most about the time you spend together? What do you enjoy the least? How often do you visit them and how often do they visit you? Do they have kids? Does that make it easier or harder for you to spend time with them? What influence do they have on your kids (if you have them)? How do they make you feel?

Not surprisingly, my own experience in this Subdi closely mirrors that of the Aunts & Uncles Subdi. Namely, we spent more time together when we were kids, less as young adults, and even less as old adults. I'm not sure I really like the term "old adults," but you get the point. Random side note: my mom once told me that the definition of old is anyone that is 15 or more years older than you, which sounds about right to me. Also, if that's true, then we're never actually old ourselves - it's just all those other people.

Now, let's get back to cousins. At first, it was exciting to visit them as they had life milestones like graduations, weddings, and kids. However, as there became more of them (my four Cousins have a total of 11 kids of widely varying ages), and we knew how crazy our schedules were with only two kids, it became more and more difficult to get together. I wish that we could have seen them more often and gotten to know their kids better, but I understand and accept why it has happened in this way. I am hopeful that we'll reconnect more as all of the kids start to move out of the house and live away from home, but it also has to be a mutual desire, so time will tell.

I mentioned that my wife has a much larger family, which also became part of my family when we got married. Due to her grandparent's prolific procreation (6 kids), her aunts and uncles' prolific procreations (15 more kids or more depending on how you count), and the same from that group of cousins (20 or more kids depending on how you count), it may be that everyone in a certain part of Michigan is somehow related to her. It's hard enough remembering everyone's name and who they're connected to, much less trying to spend time with any of them. But there is always a potential conflict with your partner if you spend too much time visiting one side of the family vs. the other, so that is something to think about as well.

The time I have been able to spend with cousins in adult life has been very enjoyable. Visiting with them is a great way to experience other places, lifestyles, and cultures with a host you know and trust, and it is fun to be the host yourself as well. I've accepted that cousins will move in and out of our lives as a priority, and that's ok because they're family, and they will still be there when life changes and they come back into focus. That is a fundamental difference from the Friends Subdi, where you often lose them along the way as your life changes.

What is one action you could take in this Subdi that would improve your satisfaction the most?

Family: Extended

Do you have people you were told are "family," but you have no idea how they are connected to you? If yes, they most likely fall into one of those categories I was describing in the Cousins Subdi, but there are other examples as well. Let's define it as anybody who is not related to your family biologically or legally, but you consider them to be "like family." They might be second cousins, third cousins, once-removed, etc., cousin's families, in-laws families, your mom's best friend, or anyone else you consider family. As you will have observed by now, I like to keep the definitions loose to make sure they're relevant for everyone.

Who would you consider to be an extended member of your family? Why? How often do you talk with them? How often do you visit with them? Why? How often do you want to see them? Who is most important to you in your Extended family? Why? If you could only see one person from this group this year, who would it be?

In general, I have not had many if any people in my life that I would call extended family. When I was a child, we used to attend large family reunions on my dad's side of the family, but mainly the kids just played with each other while the adults talked and I don't remember much about them. As a young adult, I attended a few large family reunions of my wife's family, but mainly to make her grandparents and her happy, and I recall more latching on to my wife the entire time rather than exploring for potential new extended family members. Perhaps these were missed opportunities, or perhaps these were never meant to be life changing events.

CONTENTMENT COMMITMENT

Your Contentment

Everyone has some form of family drama or trauma. You may have parents that are divorced, had a single parent, step-parents, or no parents. You may complain about your family, feel embarrassed by their politics or religion, and have moments where you want to be as far away from them as possible. Or maybe you have suffered losses or tragedies and would give anything for one more day with them. I recommend trying to accept your family and love them with all their faults. And since it is typically impossible to know them all deeply, think about which ones make you feel the most happy when you spend time together, prioritize them, and don't feel guilty about it.

◆◆◆

"Family is family. Whether it's the one you start out with, the one you end up with, or the family you gain along the way."
-- Gloria Pritchett from *Modern Family*

◆◆◆

Your Commitment

1. If you haven't already (c'mon!), download the R3 Worksheets at **ContentmentCommitment.com/Tools** and pull out the one focused on the *Family* dimension of Contentment.
2. Now that you have reflected on each of the Subdies in the *Family* dimension of Contentment, write down your ratings, rankings, and potential actions that will improve your satisfaction in each.

CHAPTER 10

Parks and Recreation
COMMUNITY DIMENSION OF CONTENTMENT

CONTENTMENT COMMITMENT

This television show is first and foremost a comedy, but in the context of a group of people working together to try to improve their community. IMDb describes it as "The absurd antics of an Indiana town's public officials as they pursue sundry projects to make their city a better place." Rolling Stone provides a bit more insight: "A sincere, and sincerely ridiculous, ode to civil service, friendship, and breakfast foods." It is a diverse cast of characters each with their own objectives and issues, but somehow, they are able to make it work.

I like the show because it represents community in the sense that they all seem to care about each other simply because they have a shared goal. I've observed similar dynamics among people who share a sense of community through other connections as well, including hometown, high school, university, place of work, favorite sports team, favorite restaurant, shared passion for a hobby, etc. I find the unifying element fascinating in a world that seems increasingly divisive. It makes me wonder if we started conversations by finding something that unites us first, would we then be more open to hearing each other's point of view on topics on which we disagree? That's a rhetorical question, but it's fun to think about, and I encourage you to experiment with it in the places where you feel a sense of community.

The Subdies of the Community Dimension

Having made it to the sixth and final dimension (that sounds ominous!) of the Contentment Commitment framework, you know what to expect by now. We're going to need to know the Subdies. Luckily, I have them right here. They include local Businesses, Schools, Places of Worship, Arts, Entertainment, and Service. There is a lot to unpack and certainly some crossover among these Subdies. Remember, the point is to reflect on different aspects of each one to think about what brings you happiness, what you'd like to do more, and what you'd like to do less. It's not so important that we map them to specific Subdies in a perfectly consistent way.

In the same way frequent fliers can recite the safety instructions from the flight attendants on demand, by now, you could probably recite the instructions for this and every Subdi in your sleep. But in case you are dreaming about more fun things, I will remind you that I'll share a series of questions to stimulate your thoughts in each Subdi to help you rate your satisfaction in each, which in turn will help you rank the relative importance of each on your happiness right now.

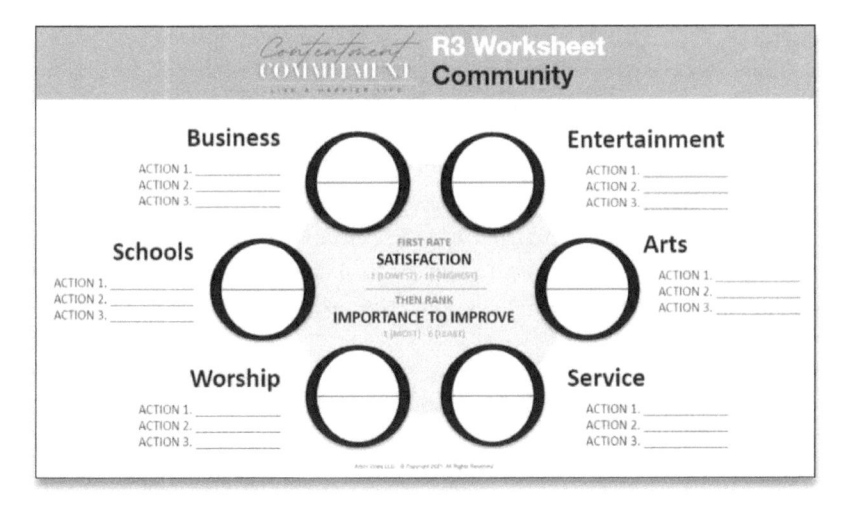

R3 Worksheet: Community worksheet with six categories (Business, Entertainment, Schools, Arts, Worship, Service), each with Action 1, 2, 3 lines. Center instructions: First rate satisfaction 1 (lowest) - 10 (highest), then rank importance to improve 1 (most) - 6 (least).

Community: Businesses

You may not think of businesses in your community as having a significant impact on your happiness. However, if you consider that restaurants, bakeries, bars, boutique shops, salons, etc, are all in this category, you might think again. Of course, some of these may be chains rather than local businesses, but even then, they are typically owned and operated locally. Often, these are the things that make a city or town unique and contribute to its character and personality. They can play a big part of the reason people travel to other places and can even be a big factor in deciding where you want to live.

What are your favorite businesses in your community? How often do you frequent them? How do you feel when you go there? What about these places brings you happiness? Is it the people, the place, or the stuff? How do you connect with the other people there? How do you connect with the owners? Does it matter to you that you are supporting your local community or is that just a side benefit? If they did not exist, would they be easy to replace? How important are these places (or places like them) in deciding where you want to live?

I only started paying attention to local businesses in my 20s, and it was not a conscious decision. I was living in Ann Arbor and liked that there were so many unique local restaurants and bars that I couldn't go to anywhere else. As I moved into my 30s, I also liked that there seemed to be clusters of places targeting students and clusters of places targeting "older" people like me. I also found myself paying more attention to which business owners seem to care about their community and sponsor events, schools, and sports teams, and I ended up frequenting them more even if I did not love their food or atmosphere as much as some others. And I liked that I could get to most of them in a 10 minute Uber ride.

When we moved to Tampa, we were in a more suburban area. While there were lots of great things about the city and surrounding area (mainly beaches and something I'm told is called the sun), I realized right away that the local businesses created a very different vibe that was not the same. There is a university there, but it did not feel like a college town. There were cool places, but I did not necessarily feel they were targeting me, and they were typically a long drive away with no other transportation options. I realized how little attention I had paid to it when we were choosing a neighborhood and house to live in, and I wished I had been more thoughtful.

As you think about your satisfaction with the businesses in your community and how you would rate their relative importance to your happiness, I encourage you to think about the broader impacts. These places can be an extremely important part of what makes you want to live somewhere or not. Also recognize that you have a role to play in ensuring they survive and thrive, and you can get happiness not only from the experience of going to them, but also knowing you are helping them continue to be a part of your community.

Community: Schools

This may be more top of mind for people with kids and probably your first thoughts turn to elementary schools, middle schools, and high schools. But keep in mind that colleges or universities can also define a community and provide lots of interesting options for adults too, including continuing education, sports, concerts and other cultural events. For the purposes of this Subdi, we'll consider all of the angles, since they all have the potential to make you feel more or less happy.

For people with kids, how important are the schools in your community to you? What characteristics are most important to you? Teacher:Student ratios? Diversity? Proximity? Facilities? Extracurriculars? College matriculation? Are you proud of the schools in your community? Why or why not? What could you do to help make them better? If you are unhappy with the schools in your community, would you move to a different neighborhood or different town to have access to ones with more of the characteristics you value most?

PARKS AND RECREATION

For those without kids, how important are the schools in your community to you? What if any role do you feel you have in supporting them? Are you proud of the schools in your community? Why or why not? If you have junior colleges, colleges or universities in your community, how do you take advantage of what they have to offer? Why?

As I reflect on my own experience, I think about my perspectives as a child and as a parent. As a kid growing up in Kalamazoo, I remember that the schools I attended had all different kinds of people and I enjoyed getting to know them. I also recall feeling sorry for some of the friends I made at other more suburban or private schools who had the false belief that my high school was a dangerous place full of drugs and gangs. Even as a kid, it was easy to see how much people feared what they did not know or have exposure to.

I also remember taking advantage of many of the benefits of growing up in a town with a community college, a college, and a large university. I got to play tennis on the same courts at Kalamazoo College that hosted the USTA Nationals every year. I remember being a ball-boy for a few years and seeing Andre Agassi play there. I also remember being dropped off at Waldo Stadium (the football field of Western Michigan University) and walking on the turf to kick field goals with my friend. And my parents took me to high school and college football, basketball, soccer, and hockey games regularly, which I thought was great. I believe I have sampled all the different types of popcorn and nachos that exist in the town.

As a parent, I find myself much more focused on how schools will impact the way my kids look at the world. My wife and I both value the diversity in the public schools, but we're realizing that we value geographic diversity as much as ethnic diversity, and we love living in a neighborhood with people from many different countries all on the same street. I've also learned that there can be a downside to being part of such a great community in that there are so many amazing kids, it is harder for our kids to stand out in sports and other activities. They are great at a lot of things and don't even know it yet because of the high quality population in which they've grown up. Of course, I may be slightly biased.

If you haven't considered how schools in your community can impact your happiness, it is worth thinking about it for a few minutes. High quality schools can make a good place to live great, and low quality schools can make a good place worse. Coming from a family of public school teachers, I feel compelled to highlight that teachers and administrators are doing the best they can with what they have, and it is better to assume the best and support them than assume the worst and complain about them. But if you do find yourself complaining too much, then either help make the change you want to see or consider changing schools to one more aligned with your vision. Even if it is a less important Subdi to you now, it may become more important to you in the future.

Community: Worship

Similar to Schools, I find that places of Worship tend to either be extremely important to people or extremely unimportant - though in this case, it does not correlate to whether or not you have kids. I've observed every combination you can imagine, including people raised in a very religious environment who have no interest in it whatsoever, to people raised in an environment with no religious focus who become very engaged in it, and many places in between. Regardless of your religious affiliation or where you may go to worship, this Subdi is about understanding how the places of worship in your community impact your happiness.

Do you attend religious services regularly? Do you want to? Why or why not? Which local places of worship have you tried? What did you like about them? What did you dislike? How do they compare with experiences you have had in other communities or other parts of your life? Does your community have one or more places of worship where you feel comfortable and connected? Do they provide emotional or financial support? Have you been exposed to any new or different places of worship in your community? Would you feel happier increasing your participation, decreasing it, or trying something new?

I was raised as a Catholic in what I would call a mixed environment in that my mom took us to church with her every week, but my dad joined us only on holidays. I was baptised and eventually confirmed after attending Sunday school for several years. I bitterly recall that the sacrament of Confirmation historically happened in 8th grade, but the year I entered 8th grade, they pushed it back to 10th grade. For better or for worse, those two extra years actually made me feel much more distant from the church than closer to it.

One exchange stands out in my mind vividly. When we first moved to Tampa, I had someone ask me a question no one had ever asked me in my entire life. And then a few more people asked me the same question in our first few months of living there. "Are you a good Christian?" I am still baffled by this as I don't know what it means. Presumably, they were asking if I attended mass regularly, thought they were being friendly, and expecting it to lead to an invitation to attend a service at their place of worship. However, it had the opposite effect on me. I have met caring and giving people who do not attend religious services regularly as well as selfish and outright mean people who do, so I do not view that as a filter. Plus, I'm more interested in the character a person demonstrates over time than how they describe themselves.

I do feel fortunate to have been exposed to all different types or religions through friends I made as a child and young adult, and I am interested to understand why others find it more or less an important part of their lives. I also feel lucky to have experienced services in churches, synagogues, and mosques. Having sampled many different types, I have yet to find one that resonates with me deeply, and as a result, religion has not played a big part in my happiness. At the same time, I struggle a bit in that our kids have attended fewer religious services than I did because of how I feel about them, and I wonder if we should do more to expand their experience with religion.

As you think about how this Subdi impacts your own happiness, I encourage you to think of it in very simple terms. If it's important to you, get more involved. The more connections you have to a community, the stronger the bond. This might mean that you find a place of worship you love and become a regular member there, but it may also mean that you sample many with the objective of gaining new friends and new perspectives. Who knows, you might even develop a good answer to the question "Are you a good Christian?"

Community: Arts

You may be used to seeing Arts & Entertainment together because newspapers (remember those?) used to always bundle the two. I've chosen to separate them in the Community dimension because there is so much included in each category, I feel it would be a disservice to talk about them as one thing. Plus, I needed a sixth Subdi for Community. We could debate what maps to Arts and what maps to Entertainment, but for our purposes, let's consider the Arts Subdi as music, theatre, dance, literature, and art galleries.

Music includes symphonies, operas, etc. Theatre includes plays and musicals. Dance includes ballet, hip hop, and many other types of live performances. Literature includes all types of writing and poetry. And art galleries include, well, everything, depending on which ones you visit. Some people love the arts. Some people don't. And a lot of people just don't know because they've never engaged with them.

Do you frequent symphonies or operas? Have you ever attended one? Why or why not? Do you attend plays and musicals? Have you ever? Why or why not? Have you visited any professional or amateur art galleries in your community?

CONTENTMENT COMMITMENT

Why or why not? How do you feel when you attend one of these? How does that compare to other things you could be doing with your limited free time? What free or low cost options exist for you to explore? What do the high schools, colleges, or universities in your community have to offer?

Keep in mind that *consuming* the arts is only one angle. Many people gain happiness from *participating* in local arts, such as community theatre or amateur art exhibitions. In addition, it is likely you have a friend or neighbor that is involved in one or more aspects, and it may make you feel good to attend an event or participate in one as a way of supporting them. Have you performed or participated in any arts in your community? Why or why not? Do you know anyone who does? If you could try one thing you haven't tried, what would it be?

In the same way my parents exposed me to many different sports at many different levels, I was fortunate to be exposed to several aspects of the arts through them and through my schooling. I attended high school plays, musicals, and band/orchestral concerts, and occasionally professional productions at Western Michigan's Miller Auditorium. As a member of my high school choir, I got to perform in three different musical productions. I remember a class field trip to the Kalamazoo Institute of Art and thinking it was a cool building, but not having much appreciation of the art inside it. I did not attend a ballet until my wife tricked me into it on a trip to New York City just a few years ago.

I can't say that I loved all the experiences, but as we always ask our children, "What if you never tried the things that you love most right now?" You would be missing out! In this space, I can only recommend that you experiment and make a point to try things you have never tried. At worst, you learn it is not for you, and at best, you discover a new passion. Either way, it usually brings some form of joy.

I am amazed how often I discover people's interest in various arts, their talents, and how they continue to stay connected to them in different ways. In my opinion, this is one of the areas that is most commonly under-nourished. If you feel unfulfilled in the Culture Subdi of the Self dimension, getting involved in your local arts community is a great place to start to make connections and be inspired to further explore your own interests.

Community: Entertainment

Ok, so if Arts includes music, theatre, dance, literature and art galleries ... then what's left for Entertainment? A lot, actually. Sports, music concerts, comedy shows, museums, bingo. Whatever floats your boat. We'll exclude things like hiking, biking, and canoeing/kayaking at local parks because we talked about those in relation to exercising on your own or with friends, but you could make an argument for including them since they can be a form of entertainment. Also consider that your community may offer sports, music concerts, and comedy options in professional and amateur settings which can provide even more options. I have not yet experienced professional bingo, but I did see axe throwing on ESPN recently, so it can't be far behind.

Do you attend professional or amateur sporting events in your community? Have you ever attended one? Why or why not? Do you attend live music concerts of bands touring in your town? Do you attend live music concerts of local bands? Have you ever? Why or why not? Does your community have live comedy shows or Improv? If yes, have you tried it? Why or why not? What other forms of entertainment do you enjoy? Going to the movies? Casinos? Bowling? Mini-golf? What types of Entertainment do you enjoy the most? Why? If you only had time to enjoy one of these each month, which would you choose?

In my own experience, I have found that I enjoy different types of entertainment with different people, and that my preferences keep changing over time. I have always enjoyed attending live sporting events, from the days growing up watching high school, university, and semi-pro sports in Kalamazoo, to when I regularly traveled internationally for work and was able to attend live soccer matches in all of the biggest leagues in the world. Then, after our kids were born, I got more pleasure in family activities like going to the dinosaur museum or hands-on museum, playing mini-golf, and bowling. The activities we could all do together became more fun than those I did on my own or with friends. And now that my kids are older, I find myself rediscovering more entertainment with friends than family.

I also used to attend many music concerts. I vividly remember my first ever concert at Wings Stadium in Kalamazoo. New Edition was the headliner with Al B. Sure and Bobby Brown performing first. I was as far away as you could possibly be, but I still loved it. I sampled lots of different types of music in different places with different people, but I always felt invigorated by the live performances, especially in smaller venues. As we get older, my wife and I continue to enjoy concerts - less frequently, but now with much better seats because we love the experience of being close. And because of her celebrity crush on Ricky Martin, we have attended several of his concerts in various locations, and that might have something to do with why we need to be as close to the front row as possible.

It doesn't really matter what forms of entertainment you are into. What is important is that you know what you enjoy the most and prioritize it. If you don't know what you enjoy the most, I recommend continuing to sample new forms of entertainment until you do. It is likely that you do some of these activities on your own, some with friends, some with family, and some with strangers who share your passion for the same team, band, etc. If you reflect on which ones bring you the most happiness, you may find that it is as much about who you are doing it with as it is the thing you are actually doing. It's fun to do things with people who love doing them as much as you do.

Community: Service

The word service may evoke different associations for different people, but for the purposes of this Subdi, we'll think of it simply as organizations that exist to help people, animals, and places in your community. From a people perspective, these often include organizations that provide food, shelter, protection or medical support to various groups such as disadvantaged youth, abused, seniors, veterans, or the homeless. The Humane Society and other similar entities seek to provide the same types of support for animals in need. And there are typically places in every community which are available to all, but they only exist because a subset of the people in the community give time and money to create and or maintain them. This could include outdoor places such as parks, lakes, and rivers, as well as indoor places like museums, theatres or public performance venues.

Examples of community service might include participating on a local government council, acting as a board member in a local sports league or theatre group, volunteering to help keep local parks clean and safe, donating time or money to local schools, or supporting local charities, to name a few. Paid or unpaid, if it is something that you do that helps improve or maintain your community, it is part of this Subdi.

What community service organizations exist to support the people, animals, and places in your community? What people do you know in your community that benefit from local community service organizations? Neighbors? Friends? Relatives? Which organizations do you feel a personal connection to? Why? How do you support them? Do you regularly use places in your community supported by service organizations? What do you do to support them? How does it make you feel when you support these organizations? If you only had time or money to support one, which one would you choose? Why?

This is an area where I have participated very little for most of my life but started to become more engaged in recent years. For a long period of my life, I could not really have told you what community service organizations existed where I live. I felt too busy with work to be able to give any of my very limited free time to volunteering, and after our kids were born, it seemed there was even less time to give, and I felt I needed to reserve as much of it as possible for sleep. As a result, I gave money rather than time. However, I paid little attention to whether the service organization was local or not and more attention to having a personal connection. For example, my paternal grandmother died of Alzheimer's, so I would consistently give to organizations pursuing a cure or better treatment options.

I also lived vicariously through my wife. In her profession as a social worker, she provided counseling support to disadvantaged youths and seniors. After she stopped working to stay at home with our two young sons, she constantly volunteered at their schools and other local organizations. Rightly or wrongly, I felt like I supported this indirectly by making enough money that she did not have to work, so this also made me feel I was doing my part. But frankly, I mainly felt guilty that I should probably be doing more, though without a strong connection to any local organizations, I didn't want to just write more checks to places and people I'd never seen.

As our young boys became teenagers, it occured to me that I probably had set a very poor example in this space as they did not see me give any time to community service and had no visibility to the money we donated. I was concerned that they would perceive this to mean that my wife cared about helping others and I did not. I also felt like they needed to have some experiences for themselves and that it could be a fun thing to do as a family. Inspired by the efforts of a friend's daughter (thanks McKee family!), this led to the most rewarding experience I've had in this Subdi.

A couple of years back, I challenged my wife and my two sons to research local community service organizations and select three to which they felt a personal connection. Along with my own three choices, this gave us 12 local community service organizations to support and experience - one per month. We were required to be physically present rather than raising funds or just writing a check. Whoever made the selection was in charge of identifying when and how we would volunteer and make all of the arrangements. While this was much more difficult than I thought, it was insightful to see what each person was drawn to and the reasons why. It was also fun to see them getting creative with their ideas and amazing to observe them while they volunteered to see how it made them feel.

If I can say it without sounding too preachy, I believe it is important to support the things you care about rather than assuming/hoping others will do it for you. It not only makes you feel good and increases the chances that the things that bring you happiness in your community will continue to be there, but it also creates opportunities to make connections with other people that share this passion and/or benefit from it. There are many different ways you can participate in community service organizations where you live, most of which only cost you a bit of your time. For those like me, you may be surprised about how good it makes you feel.

PARKS AND RECREATION

Your Contentment

With so many opportunities to feel connected to the community in which you live, it can be hard to know where to start. When you think critically about the happiness you get from each Subdi and start to explore some of them you have never tried, you get smarter about what you can give and what you can get to feel proud about your community and your place in it.

◆◆◆

"Treat yo' self."
-- Tom Haverford & Donna Meagle from *Parks and Recreation*

◆◆◆

Your Commitment

1. If you haven't already (shame!), download the R3 Worksheets at **ContentmentCommitment.com/Tools** and pull out the one focused on the *Community* dimension of Contentment.
2. Now that you have reflected on each of the Subdies in the *Community* dimension of Contentment, write down your ratings, rankings, and potential actions that will improve your satisfaction in each.

CHAPTER 11

Survivor
MAKE THE COMMITMENT

SURVIVOR

I had a harder time than I expected coming up with a popular TV series that represents commitment in the way I wanted. *The Bachelor* and *The Bachelorette* are allegedly about commitment, but I'm not aware of any relationships that started on that show which are still going, so it seems like a poor example to follow. *Survivor* isn't perfect either, but it has some aspects we can connect with for this topic. I watched the first few seasons of it when reality TV was a relatively new concept, and it ran 40 seasons over 20 years, so the show in and of itself is a survivor.

◆◆◆

Commitment: the state or quality of being dedicated to a cause, activity, etc.

◆◆◆

For those uninitiated, *Survivor* brings together sixteen (supposedly average) Americans in a remote and challenging setting for 39 days. Initially, they live as two separate and competing tribes which eventually merge into one, but then ultimately it is everyone for themselves. Along the way, there are challenges for simple pleasures and immunity. Every three days, those without immunity face tribal council where one person is voted off of the island. At the end of day 39, there is only one survivor left who leaves the island with $1,000,000.

In the context of the Contentment Commitment, there are a few relatable qualities. The contestants put themselves in an uncomfortable and unknown environment and challenge themselves to make connections with people where there is mutual benefit. Ultimately, the combination of perseverance and purposeful strategy is rewarded. Each of the dimensions of Contentment have uncomfortable spaces with people that may be known or unknown and continue to change over time. We navigate these relationships trying to prioritize those that are mutually beneficial and we persevere as our situation changes. The more thoughtful and strategic we are in this approach, the more we will be rewarded.

Of course, we would rarely think of our daily lives in those terms, but that is part of the reason for leveraging the Contentment Commitment. Up to now, the primary focus has been on thinking through all the dimensions of Contentment

CONTENTMENT COMMITMENT

(36 Subdies to be exact if you're counting at home), reflecting on your satisfaction with each, and ranking them according to what is most important to improve right now. Now is the time to act and commit.

In this part of the process, you will reflect, rate, and rank across the 6 overall dimensions of Contentment. You will review the actions you have identified that would improve your satisfaction in each, and prioritize the ones which will have the biggest impact on your happiness overall. Then, I will ask you to formally commit to a small number of them with a simple contract and a trusted friend or family member. This is where it all comes together!

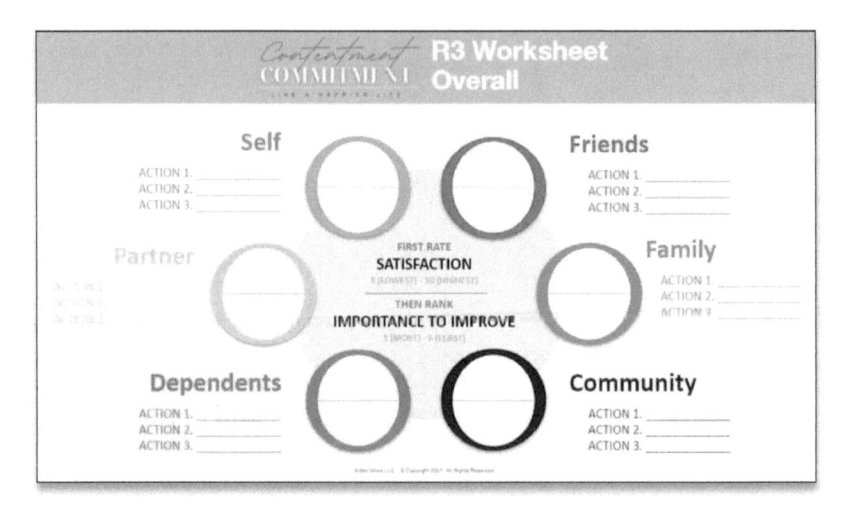

Your Reflections

If you have been completing your R3 Worksheets for each dimension of Contentment as you go, now is the time to pull them out again. If you have not been completing them along the way, I recommend completing them before trying to rate and rank the 6 dimensions of Contentment. At a minimum, it is worth the time to help inform your overall rating and ranking. While it is a healthy and valuable exercise to think about what actions you could take that would improve your satisfaction in each Subdi, we ultimately will be prioritizing them and committing to a small number of them. So don't worry about it if you have not completed that part yet.

Your Ratings

As you think about your satisfaction rating for each of the 6 dimensions of Contentment overall, please remember there is as much art as there is science in this part of the process. You are attempting to establish a baseline measurement for how you are feeling about each right now, and there is no standard or precise methodology to measure feelings. The good news about that is that there is no right or wrong way to complete your ratings. As long as you believe they represent your feelings as reasonably accurately as possible, then you have succeeded.

That having been said, I realize some people can feel stuck at this stage without a bit more guidance, so I will share some for those who want it. Across a large sample size, people who rate their satisfaction as 8, 9, or 10 typically describe themselves as feeling very happy or mostly happy and tend to have scores in this range across most of the Subdies. People who rate their satisfaction as 1, 2, or 3 typically describe themselves as feeling very unhappy and tend to have scores in this range across most of the Subdies. People who rate their satisfaction as 4, 5, 6, or 7 typically have some aspects in which they are content and other aspects in which they would like to improve. While their ratings across the Subdies can be all in this range, it is more common to see some higher, some lower, and some in this range.

Again, there is no right or wrong way to rate them, so please go with whatever feels right today because months from now, after you've made the changes to which you've committed, we'll ask the same question about how you are feeling then. Without further adieu, let's review each of the 6 dimensions of Contentment and assign a satisfaction rating.

In the Self dimension, we explored your satisfaction in the Professional, Wellness, Financial, Creative, Cultural, and Spiritual Subdies. As you look at your ratings for each of them, are they mostly low, mostly high, or mixed? What are your thoughts on your rating for the Self dimension overall?

In the Partner dimension, we delved into your satisfaction in the Subdies of Dating, Intimacy, Responsibilities, Financial, Parental, and Communication. As you reflect on your ratings for each of them, are they mostly low, mostly high, or mixed? Think about how this informs your rating for the Partner dimension overall.

In the Dependents dimension, we stimulated your thinking about your satisfaction in the Subdies of Providing, Teaching, Playing, Experimenting, Socializing and Communicating. As you look at how you rated each of those, are they mostly low, mostly high, or mixed? What does that suggest for your rating of your satisfaction in the Dependents dimension overall?

CONTENTMENT COMMITMENT

In the Friends dimension, we dove deep into Subdies of Talking, Visiting, Going Out, Exercising, Traveling, and Changing. Reflecting on the ratings in each, are they mostly low, mostly high, or mixed? How would you rate your satisfaction in the Friends dimension overall?

In the Family dimension, we asked questions about the relationships you have and the relationships you want with your Grandparents, Parents, Siblings, Aunts & Uncles, Cousins, and Extended family. Looking back at your ratings and rankings for each, how would you rate your satisfaction in the Family dimension overall?

In the Community dimension, we investigated the impact of local Businesses, Schools, Places of Worship, Arts, Entertainment, and Service on your happiness. Looking back at your ratings for each, are they mostly low, mostly high, or mixed? How would you rate your satisfaction in the Community dimension overall?

Your Rankings

If you have already been doing this for the Subdies in each dimension, then this will be a relatively easy exercise for you since the process is the same. If you haven't done that yet, I recommend doing it now as it will help you identify the specific areas in which actions you can take will have the biggest impact on your happiness. And it will make this step easier.

As with the satisfaction ratings, there is some art with the science. The downside is that there are no step-by-step instructions for you to follow that will reveal the "correct" answer. The upside is that there is no right or wrong way to do it, so you can't go wrong. If that is enough guidance for you to rate them from most important to change to least important to change, then please continue. If it is not, then I will make a suggestion to keep you moving forward.

A simple way to get started is to ask yourself, "If I could only make an improvement in one of the 6 dimensions this year, which one would have the biggest impact on my happiness?" Only you can answer that. There is no formula or algorithm to answer for you. Don't bother asking Alexa or Siri as they can't help with this one either. Once you've answered, ask yourself the same question with the remaining five, and so on. This is one of the most difficult parts but one of the most important parts as well. There are no ties. You will end with the 6 dimensions ranked from 1 (most important to improve right now) to 6 (least important to improve right now).

Some people struggle with this part because they misunderstand the objective. As a reminder, you are not ranking how much you *care* about each dimension relative to each other. You are not deciding if you care about yourself or your partner more. Nor are you trying to decide if you value your relationship with your partner more than your relationship with your kids or pets. You are simply trying to prioritize what needs most attention *right now* or, said differently, what is making you most happy or unhappy *right now*.

Once you have completed an initial pass at the rankings, I encourage you to go back and look at your ratings for each dimension. Does the ranking make sense in the context of the rating? Again, there is no right or wrong; however, it is more common that the dimensions which have the lowest satisfaction ratings tend to be the ones that are ranked most important to improve right now. Of course, there are situations in which this is not the case. The purpose of this quality check is to make your ratings and your rankings tell the same story. When you review, does it make sense to you intuitively? If yes, great. If not, cycle through this part of the process until it does.

This is also a good time to remind you about the concept of leveraging your strengths vs. focusing on "fixing" your opportunities for improvement. In many employer's performance management processes, employees receive feedback highlighting their strengths and opportunities for improvement. It is common for employees to focus on how to improve, but it is often overlooked on how to better leverage their strengths. There is a school of thought which suggests that higher performance is more likely to be achieved by better leveraging your strengths than by disproportionally focusing on your opportunities for improvement.

In the same spirit, consider that you may get more happiness maintaining a high satisfaction rating in a dimension that is very important to you than you do from improving your satisfaction in a dimension that is less important to you. So if there is an action that supports that objective, consider prioritizing it.

Your Priorities

If you have been completing your R3 worksheets along the way, then you have already captured lots of ideas of actions you could take to improve your satisfaction. If you listed one for every Subdi, that's 36 potential actions. If you listed three for every Subdi, that's 108. Yikes! If you listed none, that's embarrassing. Just kidding, but you will need more than zero to move past this section.

CONTENTMENT COMMITMENT

For those that have zero actions listed, the good news is you do not need to generate 108 ideas right now. In fact, if you consider that you will commit to just three to five changes at a time, you probably only need to generate 10 or so. For those with zero actions so far, I recommend adding actions for the dimensions of Contentment you ranked as being a 1, 2, or 3 most important to improve. Within those, focus on the Subdies that you ranked as being a 1, 2, or 3 most important to improve. If you come up with 1 action for each, then you'll have 9 to choose from, and you'll most likely have some with more than one action.

Remember the quote I shared earlier about how "it's simple to create something complex and complex to create something simple"? Well, we have taken all of the data from everyone who has ever used the Contentment Commitment framework (or at least the ones who shared their ratings and rankings) and used it to create a Priority Matrix. It's purpose is simple: to make it as easy as possible for you to decide, among all of the items you have listed which could improve your happiness, which ones should you commit to doing?

A picture is worth a thousand words, but since some people are visual and others prefer an explanation, I'll share both a picture and a thousand words (give or take). Hopefully at least one of them resonates with you.

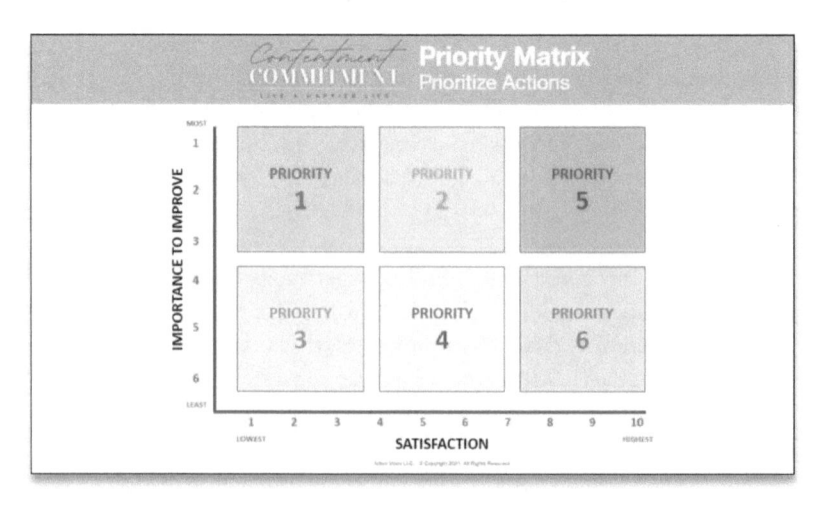

Priority 1 includes any dimension you rated as 1, 2, or 3 most important to improve AND you gave a satisfaction rating of 1, 2 or 3. In other words, if something is really important to you and you are very dissatisfied with it, doing something about it will have the most significant impact on your Contentment and is most critical to live a happier life. If you have a dimension of Contentment in this zone, I recommend committing to the one action you think

SURVIVOR

will help the most. If you have 2 or 3 dimensions that fall into Priority 1, then I recommend including one action for each of them. This is where you will get the biggest improvement in your overall satisfaction.

Priority 2 includes any dimension you rated as 1, 2, or 3 most important to improve AND you gave a satisfaction rating of 4, 5, 6, or 7. In layman's terms, we are talking about things that are very important to you and you are feeling just ok about them. If you had no dimensions of Contentment in Priority 1 (and therefore no actions in Priority 1), then Priority 2 will offer the biggest improvement in your overall satisfaction. If you had one or two dimensions of Contentment in Priority 1, then you may want to reduce the number of actions in Priority 2 proportionally. If you had 3 dimensions of Contentment in Priority 1, then I recommend committing to only one from this zone.

Priority 3 includes any dimension you rated as 4, 5, or 6 most important to improve AND you gave a satisfaction rating of 1, 2, or 3. While you are very dissatisfied with these items, you have also indicated that they are less important to you to improve. As a result, we typically only see people committing to actions identified here if they have not already identified 4-5 from Priority 1 and Priority 2. If somehow you had no items in Priority 1 or 2, then I recommend a maximum of 2 actions from this zone. They will help you live a happier life, but will have a less significant effect than those in Priority 1 and 2.

Priority 4 includes any dimension you rated as 4, 5, or 6 most important to improve AND you gave a satisfaction rating of 4, 5, 6 or 7. These are the dimensions of Contentment that are less important to you to improve, and you are feeling ok about them, so they will offer the smallest improvement in overall satisfaction of any of the actions you could take. Regardless of the number of actions you have from Priority 1, 2 and 3, I recommend committing to at most 1 action from this zone - and only if you do not have items in Priority 1 and 2.

Priority 5 includes any dimension you rated as 1, 2, or 3 most important to improve AND you gave a satisfaction rating of 8, 9, or 10. This is the happy zone. These are the dimensions of Contentment most important to you and you already have high satisfaction in them. Essentially, the action here is to not screw it up. Nearly all of the time this means you just need to keep doing what you're doing and therefore there are no new actions to commit to. As a result, I recommend committing to no actions in this zone unless it is required to maintain the rating.

Priority 6 includes any dimension you rated as 4, 5, or 6 most important to improve AND you gave a satisfaction rating of 8, 9, or 10. These are the dimensions of Contentment that are less important to you to improve, and you are feeling very satisfied with them, so why would we change anything here?

It would be easy to add complexity in the form of weighted variables or factoring in expected future rating based on committed action, but this would provide only incremental precision on potential impact at the cost of confusing a large portion of the people who are just trying to prioritize a list of possible actions. I recognize the option but have intentionally limited the guidance to the Priority Matrix to keep things simple.

As a reminder, the Priority Matrix is a guide for people who need it or want it. If you have a preferred method of narrowing your list to three to five actions that you think will have the biggest positive effect on helping you live a happier life, then go for it. Some people like to go with their "gut" and that's fine. What's important is you rationalize the short list in some way and are confident about your ability to achieve them before committing. Did I mention there is art with the science?

Your Contract

Did you know that, according to a 2018 article in *Inc.*, you are 42 percent more likely to achieve your goals if you write them down? As we near the end of the process, your Commitment takes center stage. Do you hear Vince Lombardi (from Chapter 4) whispering in your ear? To make it as easy as possible for you, I recommend you use the C3 Form (Contentment Commitment Contract) available on ContentmentCommitment.com/Tools. This is the contract you are making with yourself to follow through on the changes you have identified that will have the biggest impact on helping you live a happier life. Let's walk through it together to make sure everything is clear.

> **C3 Form — Contract**
>
> I, _____, am committed to take the following actions to **Live a Happier Life** starting on _____ and completing by _____.
>
> ACTION 1. _____
> ACTION 2. _____
> ACTION 3. _____
> ACTION 4. _____
> ACTION 5. _____
>
> Signature _____   Witness Signature _____

From the Prioritization process, you identified actions that mapped to Priority 1, 2, 3, and 4. From those, I recommend you take a minimum of three and not more than five to enter onto your C3 Form. Start with Priority 1 and include any actions you identified in that zone first. Then do the same for Priority 2 and so on until you have between three and five.

It is important to include at least three or else it is unlikely the improvement in satisfaction will be significant enough for you to feel happier. Equally, it is important to limit yourself to a maximum of five to avoid over-committing, failing to deliver on your commitment, and possibly feeling even worse. I leave you the option to choose so that you maintain control and can dial up or down based on the degree of difficulty to deliver on the changes to which you are committing.

Once you have entered the actions onto the C3 Form, you will need to pick a timeline. Like most aspects of the framework, there is flexibility. The most common timeline used so far is one year and the most common timing coincides with New Year's resolutions. However, this should not influence your timeline selection. Your timeline depends completely on how long you expect it to take to deliver on your commitments. If they can be accomplished in 3 months or 6 months, then I encourage you to use that as your timeline. Plus, the faster you achieve results, the sooner you are living a happier life and/or running through the cycle again with the next highest level of prioritized actions.

Once you have entered your timeline and target dates, the final step is to review with a trusted friend or family member. There are studies highlighting the benefits of sharing your goals with others, as well as those cautioning against it. A recent study published in ScienceDaily titled "Share your goals - but be careful whom you tell" concludes "in most cases you get more benefit from sharing your goal than if you don't - as long as you share it with someone whose opinion you value." So please, ask someone who supports you and wants to help you achieve your goals. Avoid people who think it is a silly exercise or do not take your commitment seriously. If you're able, I recommend doing it in person and making a mini-event out of it. Think of it as a formal signing event and something to be celebrated. I reviewed mine with my wife and we discussed it over a bottle of wine, but please incorporate whatever works best for you to create the right atmosphere.

When you are together, share with them how you are feeling as it relates to the 6 dimensions of Contentment. Let them know that you have been thoughtful about what makes you happy and purposeful in committing to the actions you think will have the most significant positive effect in helping you live a happier life. Ask for their help to keep you focused and to check in with you about it from time to time. I also recommend thanking them in some way so they feel some accountability for helping you achieve your goals.

Once you have shared the context and reviewed the specific actions and timelines, sign the C3 Form and ask them to do the same as a Witness. And then ... smile! You have made it farther than many others, and you are taking a comprehensive and targeted approach to changing your life for the better. As long as you keep your commitment, you should expect to reap the rewards by the end of your timeline.

SURVIVOR

Your Contentment

Congratulations on making it this far! You have a plan, you have committed to specific actions in a specific timeline, and you are now on the path to living a happier life. This is the most exciting part! Now that you are all fired up, you just need to keep the flame burning. The sooner you start the actions, the sooner you will feel the difference. I recommend reading the final chapter now, but also to come back to it and read it again at the end of your Commitment timeline.

◆◆◆

"In this game, fire represents your life. When your fire's gone, so are you."
-- Jeff Probst from *Survivor*

◆◆◆

Your Commitment

1. If you haven't already (but of course you have by now), download the R3 Worksheets at **ContentmentCommitment.com/Tools** and pull out the one focused on the *Overall* dimensions of Contentment.
2. Now that you have reflected on each of the 6 dimensions of Contentment, write down your *Overall* ratings and rankings.
3. Download the Priority Matrix and C3 Form at **ContentmentCommitment.com/Tools**. Use the Priority Matrix to help narrow your list of potential actions to the three to five that will have the most significant impact.
4. Use the C3 Form to formally Commit to taking those actions.

CHAPTER 12

Glee
LIVE A HAPPIER LIFE

What are the first television shows that come to mind when you think of happiness? It likely depends on your age and how much TV you watch, but for many of a certain age, it is *Happy Days*. That didn't work for me because I had a tough time seeing what exactly "The Fonz" had to do with being happy. You might make the same argument about *Glee*, but I like that it is more recent if not more popular, and I like the underlying theme of the show. Also, one of the cast members (Darren Criss) has ties to Ann Arbor, so I have to represent locally where I can.

Paraphrasing the description on IMDb, the storyline for *Glee* centers on how the new director of McKinley High School's failing Glee Club tries to rejuvenate it along with his failing love life. The series follows the oddball mix of eager and ambitious student members as they compete in the choir competition circuit to try to win the nationals. Along the way, they also have to deal with the tough and cruel realities of their school, and the school's sabotaging cheerleading coach. More relevant for the Contentment Commitment is the unofficial tagline: "A biting comedy for the underdog in all of us."

Different episodes focus on different characters' struggles with self-identity, their love life with partners, and their interactions with family, friends, and their community. Hopefully those dimensions are ringing a bell at this point. I also like it for this purpose because (spoiler alert) they accomplish all of their group and individual goals in the end. Let's see if we can do the same!

"Don't Worry, Be Happy"

A chapter anchoring to Glee better have some musical references, and none seems more appropriate than Bobby McFerrin's classic from the late 1980s. For those of a younger vintage, perhaps you can better connect with Pharrell's "Happy" from 2013. Either way, the point is the same: be happy! That may sound overly simple or even silly, so let me elaborate a bit.

During my time working at Accenture, the best leaders understood the importance of celebrating success. If you spend months or even years of your life trying to make something happen, and then you finally achieve your goal, it is important to pause for a moment to reflect on your accomplishment and celebrate it. You should feel proud, happy, and successful. You challenged yourself to do something you weren't sure you could do, but then you actually

CONTENTMENT COMMITMENT

did it. You probably had some bumps in the road and moments you questioned yourself, but you did it. That takes determination and perseverance. Enjoy the moment.

There is a quote from Dr. JM Perry (referenced in Chapter 3 as part of the inspiration for the Contentment Commitment) that I often find myself using: "Wisdom is the intersection of experience and reflection." Everyone has experiences, but not everyone takes time to reflect on them. The more experiences you have and the more you reflect on them, the more wisdom you gain. Once you have committed to changes meant to help you live a happier life, I encourage you to regularly reflect on how you are feeling and why. Does it seem to be working? Do you feel happier? Why or why not? Are there simple tweaks you could make that would accelerate or amplify the impact of your changes?

Whether there were one or two people who were most instrumental in your change journey or you were supported by a village of family and friends, it is important to show appreciation to everyone who helped you achieve your goals. Perhaps your partner made some changes to their routine or lifestyle to try to help you. Thank them. Perhaps some of your friends supported you emotionally and provided the encouragement you needed to keep going. Thank them. Perhaps members of your family helped you better understand why you have different quality relationships with different parts of your family. Thank them. Thank anyone who helped you in a meaningful way and let them know you appreciate their support. Only good can come from this.

You also have a responsibility to pay it forward. If something helps improve your life in a meaningful way, there is a chance it might help improve someone else's life in a meaningful way. Help them. Not in a pushy, salesy way but by finding the right moment. Have you ever had success with a diet and told everyone you know that "you have to try this diet"? Most likely it was received with resistance and suspicion about your motives. At the same time, if someone said to you, "I noticed you have lost weight and kept it off - what's your secret?" then they are in a position where they are ready to receive your information.

Just because my aspiration is to help as many people live a happier life as possible doesn't mean it needs to be your aspiration. However, you can help by sharing your experiences and feedback in places where your friends, family, and co-workers are most likely to notice it. And if you include the **#ContentmentCommitment** hashtag, then I can see it too and help amplify your voice further. The more people see the Contentment Commitment driving real results, the more curious they will become, and the more likely they are to try it.

And while it will be more life-changing for some than others, the more people who try it, the more people we can help live a happier life.

Whatever your preferred approach, please do share your experiences with others who you think might benefit from it. Whether that takes the form of a referral, gifting, choosing it for your book club discussion, or anything else you come up with, I appreciate your help to spread the word. Banner ads only go so far. And if you somehow have a horrible experience with it, please let me know, so we can continue to evolve and improve the framework for others who will try it in the future. Feedback is a gift, but positive feedback is a nicer gift to receive than negative feedback. You won't hear that at work!

"Can't Stop the Feeling"

Justin Timberlake's 2016 hit is a feel-good song that wants you to dance. You have completed all of the Reflect, Rank & Rate (R3) Worksheets, you have reviewed and prioritized all of the actions you could take to improve your satisfaction in each dimension of Contentment, you have made the Commitment to take those that are most important for your overall satisfaction, you have persevered for months and achieved the goals that you set, and you have paused to celebrate your success, thank those you helped, and shared your experiences with others who might benefit from them. You're feeling good. Are you done?

That's up to you. Just as some people will commit to change in a timeline of 3 months while others will have a 6 or 12 month target, some people will complete the Contentment Commitment cycle once and stop while others will run through multiple cycles. It really depends on the timelines you are using, the success you are having, and the amount of change required for you to live a happier life. Some need a little change to feel happier and some need a lot.

I would make an analogy to budgeting for your personal finances. If you have never done it before, you will benefit from detailed micro-management for some period of time. This helps you understand aspects that might have been overlooked when you weren't managing monthly income and expenses closely or tracking spend in specific categories. It might feel strange or challenging in the beginning because it is different, as my wife will be happy to attest based on her opinion of how we managed our finances in the early days. However, once you have run the process enough times that it becomes a habit, then you can relax some of the structure and rigor because you are essentially doing it without having to micro-manage.

My advice is to continue to set new goals and commit to changes for as many cycles as needed until it becomes a habit and you find yourself essentially doing it without the formality of the R3 Worksheets, Priority Matrix, and C3 Forms. I do however suggest that you continue to complete a Commitment Contract every time and share it with someone who will hold you accountable. For some reason, that seems to make a difference for a lot of people.

Remember, if you are feeling happier and you stop the formal process, that is a good thing, and it doesn't mean that you will stop feeling happier. And as you encounter events in your life that impact your happiness, you can always come back to it. I can't speak for Justin Timberlake, but I suspect he might tell you to just dance, dance, dance.

"A Change is Gonna Come"

In his 1964 classic protest song, Sam Cooke was singing about his struggle and of those around him as it related to the Civil Rights Movement as Black Americans fought for equality. It seems just as relevant now with the Black Lives Matter movement highlighting the continued struggle. In the context of Contentment Commitment, I also like it because it is a song with purpose.

My purpose is to try to help as many people as possible live a happier life. I believe that is most likely to happen at scale by integrating it into existing employer Wellness Programs. As a result, this opportunity should be of particular interest to Human Resources professionals who consider themselves to be leaders among their peers.

The value of supporting employees' physical health has already been recognized and resulted in increased productivity via reduced sick days and reduced healthcare costs for both the company and the individual. That means the same headcount can deliver more revenue, or less headcount is required to deliver the same revenue. A company that is not continuously increasing revenue and profitability is one that is going out of business, so anything HR can contribute to those company-wide success measures is welcomed.

More recently, many employers have begun investing in the mental health of their employees as well, and they have incorporated these services into a more holistic Wellness Program. In addition to further increasing productivity, this also typically raises Employee Engagement, or happiness at work. Towers Watson, Mercer, and other HR consulting firms have established a widely accepted link between Employee Engagement and business performance which has led to an ongoing focus on the topic. Leading organizations understand intuitively that happiness in life (Contentment) influences happiness at work.

Therefore, happiness in life influences business performance as well.

Consider the following examples. If an employee has recently started caring for a new dependent (child, pet, or aging parent), how would you expect this to impact their productivity? If an employee has gained weight or not been able to visit family or friends because they feel too busy at work, how do you expect this would impact their retention? If an employee is on the brink of divorce or a breakup with a longtime partner, how do you expect it would impact their engagement?

This creates an opportunity for leading organizations to enhance existing Wellness Programs with tools and services aimed at improving employees' happiness overall - including both happiness at work (Employee Engagement) and happiness in life (Contentment). The primary reason this is an underserved market is because there is a lack of agreement on how to measure the results. And if your first thought is happiness can't be measured, then I would ask what you think is being measured with Employee Engagement. Contentment Commitment is a simple framework which helps establish a baseline measure, set targets for improvement, identify actions to deliver on the targets, and monitor performance to ensure the targets are achieved.

What do you believe is the relationship between happiness at work and happiness outside of work? What are your HR leaders doing to help? What do you want them to do? How can you give this topic more visibility at your place of work? If your employer has yet to explore anything in this space, only good can come from piloting a contentment program and observing the impact.

"I Hope You Dance"

Like most great songs, Lee Ann Womack's #1 crossover hit from 2000 has come to mean different things to different people. For some, it is a graduation theme with parents giving advice to their children leaving home. For others, it is about moving on after the loss of a loved one. And for others, it is about persevering after a breakup. This is one of the things I like about the song as it relates to the Contentment Commitment, because living a happier life also means different things to different people. For some, it is about improving their own physical or mental well-being. For others, it is more about improving relationships with family and friends. And for others, it is about having a greater connection to their community or place of worship.

Whatever it means to you, I hope that you will do more than sit passively on the side waiting for things to get better. If the Contentment Commitment started as a song playing in the background, but is starting to make you feel the rhythm and bob your head a little, eventually you have to dance along to it. You might not be great the first time on the floor, but the more you dance, the better you will become. And how will you know if you don't try?

Your Contentment

Justin Timberlake wants you to dance. Lee Ann Womack wants you to dance. I want you to dance. Nearly all of the characters in Glee dance and they seem pretty happy. In summary, there seems to be a strong external push for you to dance. So get out on the dance floor and try out your new moves!

◆◆◆

"Life only really has one beginning and one end, and the rest is just a whole lot of middle."
-- Will Schuester from *Glee*

◆◆◆

Your Commitment

1. Celebrate your success in completing your Contentment Commitment.
2. Thank the people who helped you.
3. Share your story with others to inspire them (and use **#ContentmentCommitment**).
4. Share your story with me at **ContentmentCommitment.com/Share**.
5. Run through the cycle again if it is helpful.
6. Also, dance. Nobody else has to know, it's just between us.

ACKNOWLEDGMENTS

I never aspired to write a book, but I do aspire to try to make the world a better place - at least the parts I am able to influence within my limited reach. I am grateful to the many people who have helped make the world a better place for me.

Special thanks to Raul Alvarado and Dr. JM Perry for their roles in helping me understand and prioritize my happiness, and inspiring me to try to help others do the same. This is a gift that keeps on giving.

Thanks to Ty Sassaman, Todd Thompson, Erin Osgood, Chriss Danna, and Mike Dulworth for their support, encouragement, and honest feedback which helped take the idea from concept to reality. And thanks to the McKee Family for inspiring me to try new ways of giving.

Thanks to Rachael Holt of Rachael Holt Photography for the photo used on the book cover and website, as well as the Author photo.

Thanks to Yasmin Sara Gruss for her copy editing expertise and elevating the quality of the final version.

Thanks to my wife Jennifer and my kids Connor and Donovan for allowing me to explore and experiment with you, for your patience and trust as I try to be the best husband and father I can be, and for bestowing me with the honor of "best dad in the house."

Thanks to my family Jon and Jane, Bob and Carol, Thom and Destinee, Melinda and Scott, for your unconditional love and for providing so many different experiences which have helped me understand what happiness means to me.

Thanks to my friends old and new who have helped me understand what it means to be a good friend, and especially those that have visited and spent time getting to know my family.

Thanks to friends and colleagues who supported the book launch including Christine Bailey, Martin Barbaglia Irizar, Jonn Behrman, Charley Betzig, Vaibhav Bhushan, Heather Charron, Ashlie Collins, Bettina Daverio, Tommaso de Mol, Veerle Dero, Chad Dinzes, Soraya El Ramly, Michael Falkner, Jesper Faurholdt, Alejandra Ferraro, Mary Finch, Federica Fiorentino, Lisa Fortuna, Scott Gaudes,

Natachia George, Anoop Gupta, Shishir Gupta, Kelly Hines, Jennifer Huelsmann, Brock Isanhart, Deepesh Jobanputra, Miranda Kalinowski, Karen Kemp, Purnima Kumar, Jeanne Leeders, Lucia Lichvar, Bob Lopes, Garrett Lord, Brett Lutz, Michael Nasif, Annabel Nichols, Paul Nickodemus, Yann Ofanowski, Merve Oklap, Laura Oliver, Camila Proenca, Cristina Ramirez, David Reed, Kristen Ribero, Francesca Romana Rossi, Alejandro Santillanes, Becky Schmitt, Andrew Soane, Ahne Titus, Simone Wamsteker, Susan and Perry Warbrick, Tressa Wolford, Amanda Worthington, and Bill Ziegler. This amazing team represents 35 employers across 15 countries.

There are countless others who have helped shape my views over the years, but I would like to highlight childhood friends in Kalamazoo, classmates and friends from Kalamazoo College, colleagues and friends from my time at Accenture and Whirlpool, friends and neighbors from our time living in Tampa, and especially soccer teammates throughout the years who share a passion for the beautiful game and the global camaraderie that comes with it.

I appreciate everyone who has been a part of my journey so far, and I hope that you, your family, and your friends are able to live a happier life with or without this framework.

Printed in Poland
by Amazon Fulfillment
Poland Sp. z o.o., Wrocław